The Little Lucky

The Little Lucky

A FAMILY GEOGRAPHY

Gail Wells

The paper in this book meets the guidelines for permanence and durability of the Committee on Production Guidelines for Book Longevity of the Council on Library Resources and the minimum requirements of the American National Standard for Permanence of Paper for Printed Library Materials Z39.48-1984.

Library of Congress Cataloging-in-Publication Data
Wells, Gail, 1952-
  The Little Lucky : a family geography / Gail Wells.
     p. cm.
  ISBN-13: 978-0-87071-189-3 (alk. paper)
  ISBN-10: 0-87071-189-X (alk. paper)
  1. Wells, Gail, 1952- 2. Wells, Gail, 1952---Family. 3. Oregon--Biography. I. Title.
  CT275.W38145A3 2007
  979.5'043092--dc22
     [B]   2006039346

Oregon State University Press
500 Kerr Administration
Corvallis OR 97331-2122
541-737-3166 • fax 541-737-3170
http://oregonstate.edu/dept/press

For my mother

Contents

Acknowledgments

Kathy, Mary, Charles, Steve, Jo, Mary, Leslie, Gavin, Mary, John: *Thank you.*

The Elkins School

~~~~

The Little Luckiamute River flows off the east slope of Sugarloaf Mountain in the Oregon Coast Range, the highest of the folded purple hills you can see from our living-room window. It starts just over Fanno Ridge from what was once the logging company town of Valsetz, razed to the ground by Boise Cascade in 1984. It flows down through Black Rock, Falls City, and Bridgeport, where I used to take my sisters swimming in the rock-lined hole below the rapids next to Bridgeport School. I'd drive barefoot in my bathing suit over the back-country roads, my toes wrapped around the accelerator pedal, windows cranked down, radio cranked up, trunk lid wide open over a couple of fat inner tubes. When I came home again, I took my children to swim there.

From Bridgeport the Little Lucky takes a southeasterly sweep across the toe of Cooper Hollow and goes on to join the Big Luckiamute a little southwest of our house on Elkins Road. The joined river passes Helmick Park along the old Valley & Siletz railroad grade. (Back in the thirties, the logging company named its town Valsetz after the two ends of the rail line, conflating the names as easily as they'd couple two rail cars together.) The rail line crosses under U.S. 99, meanders across the floodplain, and empties into the Willamette a couple of miles south of Buena Vista.

On its eastern edge, the valley of the Little Lucky has broad fields of grass seed, hay, alfalfa, and pasture, interspersed with vineyards and orchards of filberts and apples. To the west, the rolling farmland grades into steeper slopes covered with young second-growth timber and patchy clear-cuts. Beyond these are tumbles of hills that look like a blue-purple rug pushed up against the wall of the horizon.

We live in what used to be the Elkins School. It sits on a three-acre parcel of the Holman Donation Land Claim in the valley of the Little Luckiamute; we call it the Little Lucky for short. The closest town is Monmouth, five miles to the north.

The schoolhouse is probably more than a hundred years old—we don't know exactly, but you can tell it's old when you go down to the basement and see the full-dimension two-by-ten clear beams holding up the floor above. You can't buy lumber like that nowadays.

Up until the 1920s there was a little town here. Children from neighboring farms came to the Elkins School. Some rode their horses and some rode the train; a spur line used to run along our eastern fence, or so says family lore. When country schools were consolidated in the 1930s and 1940s, the children went to school in town, and the Elkins School was closed.

Then came December 1941, and the Army commandeered the whole valley of the Little Lucky and several square miles of surrounding land. They needed a military base and a training ground for soldiers headed for France and Belgium, the Philippines and Leyte Gulf. The Little Lucky valley looks like the gently rolling countryside of eastern France, and so the Army must have thought it was a good place to practice war. They evacuated all the farmers on a couple weeks' notice.

They leveled a whole town to build the base. They named it Camp Adair, after Lieutenant Henry R. Adair, a native of Astoria, Oregon, who was killed in the Mexican War. They even evacuated the graveyards out along the Little Lucky, stones, bones, and all. They moved the pioneer graves to the Fircrest Cemetery, on Old Highway 99, where my grandparents and my father are buried. The weathered headstones rise behind the newer graves, whose neat plaques are set flush with the ground to accommodate the lawnmowers.

When the war was over, my grandfather and his family came back to Monmouth from Iowa, where he'd been teaching Navy pilots how to navigate. The farmers, the lucky ones, came back to the Little Lucky valley to reclaim their land. But no one claimed the Elkins School, and the school district put it up in a veterans' lottery in 1948. My grandfather drew the winning ticket, and the schoolhouse was his for one hundred dollars. This was newsworthy enough for a page-one story in the Monmouth *Herald* of April 29, 1948:

Matthew R. Thompson, former Monmouth high school principal and at present on the staff of the Oregon College of Education, joined with other veterans in drawing cantonment land not yet taken over in the name of original owners. They planned to get hold of what is known as "Poverty Ridge" and build themselves homes on it. However Mr. Thompson drew the former Elkins school house with a little less than four acres of land. He is planning to rebuild the school building into a dwelling. It had not been used as a school for a long time, its most recent use being as a community building.

The reporter does not say where Poverty Ridge is, but my guess is that the schoolhouse would have been right at home there. There are no pictures of it from that time, but it must have been a wreck—bombarded by artillery shells, bivouacked in by soldiers, inhabited at times by sheep getting in out of the weather. I don't know what my grandfather was thinking. He was a mathematician, not a carpenter. But he was a frugal man, a use-it-up-wear-it-out-make-it-do-or-do-without sort of man, and he relished a challenge. I think he regarded his winning lottery ticket as a real stroke of luck. I don't think a brand-new house would have made him happier.

I close my eyes and imagine cracked foundation walls, gaping glassless trapezoidal windows, stove-in roof beams pressing down on wall studs, wall studs canted askew from floor joists, everything leaning wrong and out of balance. Grandpa took a chance on the wrecked old school, believing—he must have believed—that with a lot of work and a little help he could turn it into a decent home.

While his neighbors along the Little Lucky rebuilt their farms and their lives, Grandpa and his sons and sons-in-law rebuilt the old school. They tore down and built up, they straightened and pushed and pulled and banged that schoolhouse into shape. I wasn't there, but I close my eyes and imagine it: my father, young and smiling and full of hope, his arms cradling a stack of two-by-fours, his huge hands skilled and gentle with the wood. I imagine

my grandfather, slightly stooped even in his forties, prying apart
the toenail joints with a crowbar, the nails screaming bright out
of the old boards, stripped of their rusty skins. I imagine decades
of schoolroom chalk and dried mud and field dust and desiccated
mouse turds rising into the air like a burnt offering.

Grandpa and Grandma turned the school into a plain,
serviceable dwelling. Their two youngest were still living at home,
and in the summertime the kids would walk across the fields and
go swimming in the Little Lucky. My mother and father were
married in that house. Our large extended family celebrated
many Thanksgivings there. My grandmother died there, and it
was there we held my father's wake.

When I was a little girl, I told my mother, "I want to live
in Grandma's house when I grow up." Later, after John and I
were married and living with two babies in a little apartment near
Seattle, and he was out of work along with a lot of people, and we
were desperate for a place of our own, my mother remembered
what I'd told her. She was ready to sell the house, she said; she'd
carry the contract and give us a good deal, so why didn't we just
move in?

It seemed a stupendous stroke of luck, and that right there tells
me that my idea of luck is pretty much the same as my Grandpa's.
And so we moved down, to a place with even fewer jobs and a
house that still had a lot wrong with it. John pumped sewage
lagoons, sold insulation, painted houses, and did his best to keep
ahead of the decay at home. I canned applesauce and put buckets
under the leaks.

What were we thinking? We must have believed that, with a lot
of work and a little luck, we could make it. We must have been
determined to hold on even when things got bad, and they did
get bad. We did our best to make a life here, in this remodeled,
rehabilitated, redeemed old schoolhouse, this slantwise structure
of family memories.

When you live in an old house, the remodeling and rehabilitating
never end. I guess the same is true when you belong to a family.
Most families are loving in their way, and most are troubled in
their way. That was the way it was with the family I come from.

Always something is not quite right; something is leaning out of balance. The incessant vocation, or burden, to *fix things up* is what this place gave me. Transformation is never quite achieved, because just when you get hold of one thing, something else gets away from you. You bang one stud into place, and another goes cattywompus. That's the way it is. That is what these stories are about.

But when that happens, something unexpected comes with it, some gentle insistent force that transforms by breaking down, by softening. And so these are also stories of acceptance; of doing what you can and letting the rest go; of learning what is precious and what is expendable; of the surprising solace of surrendering to the possible; and of gratitude for incredible good luck.

These stories reveal an intimate geography, how a place and a family are bonded to one another. They are about the power of that bond to bend and push and straighten you even as you believe you are the one doing the bending and pushing and straightening. They are about love pushing against love, about grace that rises up like a burnt offering when the seductive ideal bumps hard against the stubborn flawed goodness of the real.

Home Improvement

≈≈

John and I got to talking about the house the other morning. It was a sunny Saturday, and we were lingering over the last of the coffee. The conversation started with a newspaper article I was reading about February being a good time to dig new garden beds. I told John I thought it was time to terrace the front entryway, the way we'd talked about, but I didn't want to do it till the foundation work was done. And then, of course, there was the roof.

"I've been thinking about that," John said. He was wearing his tan Carhartt overalls and striped logger's shirt, his normal attire on a sunny Saturday. "I've been kind of waiting till the weather gets nice. We don't want to take the roof off till it dries up. And if we dig around the house now and it rains, we'll have a trench full of mud, and that's gonna be a mess."

Fine, I said, but I'm also anxious to get a decent roof on this house. I'm willing to help, I said (knowing that it is not so much my help as his muscle that gets these things done).

"Okay," said John, not minding my nagging. "Here's what we do." He dug through the pile of junk mail on the telephone table and found an envelope and a pen. He thought for a moment, tugging his beard, and then started scrawling shapes and lines on the envelope. "We dig all around the house and we pour a footing and we fill the cracks. We jack up the southwest corner and replace the foundation wall there. We replace the drainfield—that's why there's water puddling down in that corner of the basement. We lay down drain tile and backfill and do our landscaping. And then we'll have a foundation ready to support a pitched roof. We could have it mostly done by the end of the summer if we worked our tails off."

One of us has said the same thing, or nearly the same thing, many times since we moved into this house. We're going to fix up the kitchen, or tear out the leaking shower in the bathroom, or replace the wallpapered tongue-and-groove walls with sheetrock.

We're going to build a loft and paint the house slate-blue with skim-milk trim. We're going to rewire, replumb, reroof, re-floor, revamp, renew. We get all excited and we draw schematics, and we calculate how much of our friends' time and labor we can decently exploit, and we talk earnestly about property values and interest rates and building codes.

And then the sun climbs higher and the coffee gets cold, and Gavin needs a ride to baseball practice, and we go on about our ordinary business, until the next sunny Saturday.

These conversations haven't all been in vain. We have (or, mostly, John has) done quite a few things to the place. We have torn out the leaky shower and retiled the bathroom floor. We've sheetrocked and repainted some of the living-room walls. We've installed new kitchen cabinets, a new floor, and a new ceiling. We've ripped out the living-room carpet, soggy with silt and dust mites, and polished the underlying schoolroom linoleum to a cheery shine. (There is clear fir tongue-and-groove under the linoleum, but the prospect of getting down to it makes me tired.) We've built a quarry-tile hearth and bought a woodstove and painted it blue, to catch the color of the sky that comes in wavily through the rolled-glass windows.

I like my house. I like its bare floors, its dusty shafts of sunlight. I recognize it for what it is: an awkwardly proportioned, L-shaped cabin with a kitchen the size of a Pullman compartment jutting off the north side. Many things are still wrong with it. The foundation. The roof—we've re-covered it once and patched it countless times, but still it leaks; a nearly flat roof is folly in this country.

The house is not blue but yellow, one of my least favorite colors, but it's better than Harvest Gold, its color when we bought it from my mother. That was better than its first color, Government Issue Green, because my grandfather, being a Navy veteran, got the paint surplus. The loft is pure fiction. There used to be a loft in the old schoolhouse, but my grandfather took it off after his two younger children had left home. He was a frugal man, not one to harbor superfluity; he didn't need the extra floor after the children were gone, and so off it came.

John and I moved here from Seattle in 1980, desperate for a house of our own. At the time it seemed our only chance, a sort of backhanded inheritance. I had loved the place as a child, the little creek smelling of cow manure that rimmed the property, the culvert pipes under the road that you could crawl through when it was summer and the creek was down to a trickle, the wooden-seated swing down in the grove of oak trees. I loved the smell of frying bacon drifting down the stairs as I came up from my basement cot for breakfast, the storeroom with its rows of canned prunes in Mason jars and cases of government-surplus chocolate syrup labeled "Chocolate Syrup" in plain black and white.

When I came back with John, I saw the place with adult eyes. I saw the peeling beige grasscloth wallpaper and the filthy beige carpeting and the beige ceiling stains where water had come through. I saw the faults in the foundation wall, felt the bathroom floor give where the leaking shower had made a patch of dryrot a foot across. Every winter there were new leaks in the roof. We would spend weeks stepping over buckets of brownish water.

For a long time I couldn't face the question of why my mother had let it go so badly. When I saw how much effort it took just to keep abreast of the decay, I understood a little better. Mom never intended to stay here. She'd moved in after she finished graduate school, divorced, poor, with my three teenaged sisters, accepting the shelter offered by her father. Grandpa hadn't done much upkeep, either. He was in his seventies then, and the place had gotten away from him after Grandma died.

We were poor too in those days, John and I, with two small children and only odd jobs and family charity to support us. I was ashamed of the way the house looked, ashamed in the same way I used to be as a child when my father, having drunk a little more than he'd planned, would head across the street to visit the neighbor in his pajamas. Embarrassed that acquaintances would look down on me for my shabby house, or, worse, bathe me in a ruthless pity.

We could not seem to keep the weather or the bugs out. One February the power went off for a couple of days. The only heat was a fire in the crumbling basement fireplace. Cobwebs hung like shreds of moist toilet paper to the rotting mortar between the bricks. The corners of the basement floor were damp and oozing. Gavin and Mary and I toasted wienies and marshmallows and sang songs. *We are living exactly like weasels in a hole in the ground*, I thought to myself. One song we sang was "The Frog He Would A-Wooing Go." It has a chorus that goes, "With a roly-poly gammon-and-spinach, heigh-ho, says Anthony Rowley!" Gavin was five. He sang lustily, "With a roly-poly Gavin-and-spinach ..." I fought back tears of gratitude; *Thank you, God, he's not terrified, like I am.* I had to believe the kids would be okay. I did that by seeking my reassurance from them, and, sometimes, by drinking a little more than I'd planned. By the next year, when Gavin started first grade, he had developed a habit of licking his upper lip repeatedly until it was raw and bleeding. When that song comes back to me now, it brings memories unfogged by wishful thinking or alcohol, and it makes my stomach hurt.

And yet, all along, something in this place comforted and satisfied me. Even with the leaks and the cracks and the peels, I felt embraced by the house, soothed by it, deeply at home in it. There were moments of rich contentment. I sat next to the woodstove and closed my eyes and listened to the rain splash against the window glass. I watched the sun set behind the Coast Range, watched it bathe the living room in its slanting light. I sat crosslegged on the lawn on a summer night and watched an owl patrol the hedgerow.

An inheritance always comes with strings attached. You always owe, and what you owe is the owning, the acknowledgement, the guts to stand up and say, *This is who I am, this is where I come from.* I inherited this house and the loving, troubled family that came with it, and for a long time I was ashamed to own any of it. Wanting more than was offered, I took less than I needed, and I took that grudgingly, resentfully. Now—and I'm not sure why; maybe it's the resignation of approaching middle age, or maybe I've really declared peace—I can own my inheritance, accept it gratefully and without regret. I make such improvements as I can. This is my home. This is where I live.

Patchwork

In the evenings of early summer, while my family watches baseball games on the television, I've been mending an old quilt, one of the small inheritances that came with this house. It's a patchwork quilt that my grandmother pieced from five-inch squares of scrap fabric. The squares recall the shirts she made for Grandpa, the dresses for herself and her daughters and her granddaughters, her slipcovers and draperies. They're of mostly muted colors, grays and navys and small stripes and sprigs, spare and sturdy, like Grandma herself.

The quilt kept Gavin warm in bed for most of his childhood. I've been covering the worn-out patches with new ones, folding the edges under and pressing them lightly with the iron, then blindstitching them over the faded fabric that my grandmother pieced in place forty years ago. Patching the patches. The quilt now has brighter spots—I've added orange-and-gray mattress ticking and red calico to the mix.

This home of ours is pieced together from the materials at hand. When Grandpa set out to rebuild the old schoolhouse, he started by tearing off the rotting east wing and using the salvaged lumber to patch up the rest of it. Grandma put in soft-edged patches of perennials under the big maple trees out front. "Don't you dare walk on my Canterbury bells," she told us grandkids. She planted climbing roses next to the road, and laid out a big vegetable garden behind the house in neat rectangles. She raised the seedlings herself in the greenhouse Grandpa pieced together from the school's old windows.

When my mother moved in, she planted peonies, asparagus, rhubarb, rhododendrons, blueberry bushes. And since we've been here, we've added to the patchwork. Rosebushes next to the driveway. A Granny Smith apple tree in the orchard. A stairstepped patch of black-eyed Susan and California poppy and blue salvia marching up the bank to the front door, their beds edged with broken concrete from a friend's demolished driveway.

We're constantly trying to keep up with the holes and threadbare places: the roof, the foundation, the rotting bathroom floor. There are some bright new patches: a window in the bedroom wall, letting the south light in to bless us in the wintertime.

When I'm in a sour mood, I see only the bad spots. My mother's peonies—right now the blossoms are billowing out like pink sheets on a clothesline. But there's a gap in the middle of the row from the time I dug into the bed and transplanted a fistful of muddy tubers down under the lilac trees. Every spring the leaves emerge like glossy green hands from the duff, and then they sit there in the shade, stunned, rebuking me for my thoughtlessness. I'd move them back, but it's too late—I'd have to disturb the main row again. Like me, peonies would rather stay rooted in one place.

When Gavin was five, we moved him to the basement bedroom, at the other end of the house, far from the rest of the family. We thought he would enjoy having his own space, and we felt he and his sister were too rambunctious to share a room. We shouldn't have uprooted him. I remember the soggy February morning when the basement flooded, and I heard his faint voice calling, "Mom?" I looked down the stairs and saw him, wrapped in Grandma's quilt, wading barefoot through the flood water, wincing as his baby toes touched the wet gritty floor.

It seems to me that you can go at designing a garden, a home, or a life in a couple of different ways. One way is to start from an overall plan, conceiving the whole at the outset and then following a top-down logic, bullying the process along like a field marshal, making things come out exactly the way you want. It's like making a quilt with one of those intricate patterns, Log Cabin or Double Wedding Ring.

Some people seem to be good at this. I am not one of them, because every time I try it, something goes wrong—sometimes badly wrong. A patchwork approach seems a better way for me. I don't always get to choose the pieces, but I am learning to make something beautiful with the pieces I have. I don't always get to dictate the pattern, but I can watch as one emerges, and more often than not it unfolds with a grace I did not expect and could never have imagined.

Dad's Story

≫≈≈

Dad was born in a farmhouse up the Coos River in 1919, the fifth child of Hilma Ferdinanda Larsson Ahlquist Petersson and her second husband, Erland Egan Petersson. They had both emigrated from Sweden, separately, and married in Coos Bay, Oregon. It was called Marshfield then, and the town was built on boards above the tide flats. Hilma was a handsome blonde woman—I can tell this even from the black-and-white photos taken in her later life, when her expression is dour and remote. She had those striking brow ridges and deep-shadowed, light-blue eyes that you see in so many Swedish faces. I've inherited her build: tall, broad-shouldered, sturdy-legged, with large hands and feet. They named their fifth child, who would become my father, Bertil Anson, a name evoking the old country. Dad was a handsome six-footer, with blue eyes and black, curly hair. "Some Frenchman must've slipped in under the fence somewhere back along the line," he said.

The five older Peterson children (the extra "s" was lost somewhere in the New World) finished school at the eighth grade and went to work. The sixth, Eunice, finished high school and went on to the University of Oregon, where she roomed with a girl named Virginia Thompson, who became my mother. But that's another story.

Dad's father, my grandfather Erland, died when Dad was only a few months old. When he was still in grade school, Dad had a job at the dairy down the road, milking cows morning and night. That's why he had such muscled hands and arms. Once, knowing he could fly if he just had the right equipment, he built himself a pair of plywood wings and took off from the top of the barn. He plummeted to the ground with his arms straight up and the plywood banging his ears. During the summers he and Uncle Ken walked across the log rafts on the Coos River, just because they could. Then they'd jump in the river and swim awhile and compete to see who could stay underwater the longest. Dad claimed he could stay under for two minutes. "But that Ken, with his big barrel chest, he always beat me," he said. "Used to scare me to death, how long he'd stay down."

The only time his mother ever whipped him was for wasting food, throwing a heel of bread into the stove instead of eating it. Much later Dad said, obscurely, "My mother never turned loose of anything that wasn't pried out of her."

The Japanese attacked Pearl Harbor two days short of Dad's twenty-second birthday. He and Ken went into Coos Bay to enlist. They'd agreed to join the Navy, but Ken somehow ended up in the Marine Corps line. Dad said Ken did it on purpose because it was the shortest line. Dad tested for Navy officers' school, and was accepted and commissioned an ensign. He was about ready to go when the Navy found out he'd broken his neck in a tractor accident a few years before. They told him to stay home. Ken went to Iwo Jima and came back with a Purple Heart. "He got it jumping into a foxhole and cutting his butt on a beer can," said my father. He was proud of his brother.

In the months after the war, when the price of lumber was reaching the sky, he and Ken and their older brother Shafer pooled their money and built a sawmill on Coos Bay and another up Sandy Creek, near a settlement called Remote, deep in the southern Oregon Coast Range. It was the heyday of the so-called "gyppo" outfits that sprang up after the war. A couple of guys would buy a bulldozer and a log truck and get a contract to log a tract of timber. They'd saw the logs into lumber in a corrugated-steel sawmill they'd throw up on a clearing near where the timber was. Some of the lumber went to Europe, which was rebuilding itself after the devastation of the war, but most of it went to southern California to build tract houses. Millions of GIs were coming home and getting married and starting large families. The sky was the limit. The brothers dreamed of getting rich. I was only three or four, but I remember a shiny black car and a beautiful long low ranch house in Coos Bay, paneled in dark wood, built by my father's own hands.

The sawmills did all right for a while, so the brothers decided to expand. Putting up the Remote mill as collateral, they built another sawmill at Port Orford, fifty miles south of Coos Bay on the Curry County coast. We moved to Port Orford and rented a little house on Coast Guard Hill. We were within walking distance of the cliff that hung over the ocean. "On a clear day you can see Japan from here," Dad said.

Here is a piece of family legend that probably has a basis in fact. Once Dad's buddy Arnold Poage got locked up in the Port Orford jail for some drunken disorderliness or other. Dad got indignant at this. In the middle of the night he went and fetched a log truck and backed it up to the wall of the jail. He wrapped a choker cable around the bars, put the truck in gear, and drove forward. I guess he expected to pull the bars out of the window. Instead, the whole wooden side of the jail pulled loose and tipped with a splat in the mud. Arnold Poage stood open-mouthed in the gaping hole that used to be a wall, blinking like Lazarus emerging from the tomb. They still tell that story in Port Orford.

On Christmas Day of the year I turned five, Sandy Creek rose in a flood and washed out the mill at Remote. And then the price of two-by-fours plunged, and the Port Orford mill couldn't pay for itself, and my father and his brothers were broke. And then, as if that weren't enough, it turned out that Dad, who kept the books, had been paying the bills with the employees' payroll taxes, money he should have been sending to the Internal Revenue Service. He had been trying desperately to keep things running for one more day, one more day. There was a huge judgment, which none of the brothers could pay. The IRS didn't even bother trying to collect because there was nothing to collect. My dad and my uncles had sold houses, boats, everything, and poured it all into the mills.

The IRS judgment haunted my father until the day he died. For years he was afraid to buy a house, and he never afterward dared to accumulate any assets that might have tempted the IRS to come around. We moved back to Coos Bay, but the beautiful ranch house had been sold. We lived in another place that Uncle Shafer built, a duplex, comfortable but not fancy. My mother never liked it. "Come look at this, Bert," she used to say, with a *House Beautiful* magazine in her hand, its pages turned to floor plans. Uncle Shafer and Aunt Ginevra and cousins Kenny and

Judy lived downstairs. Whenever my sisters and I got too noisy upstairs, Aunt Ginevra would pound on the ceiling with a broom handle. She and my mother never got along.

Dad went to work as a retail clerk in a lumberyard, and then he got into the log-brokering business, buying and selling timber over the phone, wheeling and dealing with landowners and logging outfits and bankers and Japanese traders. There were many times, he said, when he'd buy a timber stand or a load of logs on his own faith and credit and have it delivered to one of the ships that lined the Coos Bay harbor—"and all the time I never owned one two-by-four." Most times he collected in time to cover the float. Sometimes he overextended himself. One day the phone rang, and it was the president of the bank, a Norwegian named Ryder Bugge—Dad called him Radar Boogie behind his back. "Burrrt!" boomed the president in Dad's ear. "Burrrt, you got ta come down right avay. You're t'irty t'ousand dollarss overdrawn." Dad used to tell this story in a convincing Norwegian accent, laughing at himself. "You can bet I turned white as that sheet," he said. He never told me how he got out of that one, but he did have a favorite saying: "If you can't beat 'em, dazzle 'em with footwork."

Dad used to joke that he sold rogs and rumber to the Japanese. Japanese businessmen were his best trading partners, and their accents tickled him. Many nights we'd have a Japanese ship's officer or two at our dinner table. There was not much conversation, but there was a lot of smiling and nodding, and we children were on our best behavior without being told. Our Japanese guests always brought gifts. One man, Tim Sato, became a frequent visitor and a family friend. He brought my mother a large Japanese doll in a glass case. The doll is wearing a traditional Girls' Day costume. My mother still has it.

Dad had a lot of friends. He seemed to attract eccentrics. "If there's a ding-dong anywhere in the neighborhood, he's on my lap in five minutes," he said. There was Gus Flynn, a dim, smiling man with mournful blue eyes who used to play hillbilly music on a steel guitar. Dad played a middling guitar himself, mostly Five-Foot-Two Eyes of Blue-type stuff. He thoroughly disliked hillbilly music, and besides, Gus was tone-deaf. "Can't play sweet Jesus in whole notes," Dad said disgustedly. "Just whang, whang, whang all the time."

He was friends with Martti Jumpponen, who ran the Valhalla Tavern—the Finn Church, Dad called it—at the foot of Bunker Hill, Coos Bay's Scandinavian neighborhood. Dad told a story about the time Martti Jumpponen bought a new fishing boat and was anxious to show it off. So he invited his friends Bronko Krsmanovich and Walter Wohlenschlaeger to take a ride out on the bay. They'd had a few beers, and they took a few with them. It was a windy day and the whitecaps were forming, and wouldn't you know, they were intercepted by the Coast Guard cutter. A young lieutenant came on board, "fresh out of the Academy and smart as paint," said my dad.

The officer pulled out his clipboard and demanded, "Who's the master of this vessel?"

"I am, Sir," said Jumpponen.

"Yes? And what's your name?"

Jumpponen told him. "How do you spell that?" the lieutenant demanded. Jumpponen told him. He wrote each letter, slowly, on the clipboard.

"And who are you?" asked the lieutenant, pointing with his pencil. The seas were rising, and the deck was starting to heave and sway.

"I am Walter Wohlenschlaeger."

"I see. And how do you spell that?" The lieutenant braced himself against a bulkhead and penciled down the letters. It took him a long time. He was beginning to look a little green.

"And you?"

"I am Bronko Krsmanovich."

"Ah, shit," said the lieutenant and threw down his pencil. It rolled away and vanished. "Ah, shit," he said. Snatching a pen from Martti Jumpponen's pocket, he scrawled on his clipboard, "And passengers."

Dad laughed every time he told this story. "Fresh out of the Academy! Smart as paint! 'And passengers!' "

Dad's father, my grandfather Erland, could stay sober and apparently content for six months at a stretch, but then he'd start pacing the floor at night. This restlessness was the precursor to a violent drinking binge. The liquor turned him into a different person, unpredictable and mean. After a couple of days of savage drunkenness he'd have worked the craving out of his system, and he'd sober up and be his gentle self again for a few months.

In January of 1929 Erland went on a binge with two buddies. They drank some tainted moonshine liquor, and it poisoned them. One man died, one went blind, and my grandfather went berserk and had to be subdued by five sheriff's deputies. They bound him in baling wire and put him on the night train to the state psychiatric hospital in Salem. He died of pneumonia ten days later. He was thirty-seven years old. He was cremated and his ashes stored in the state hospital because my grandmother didn't have enough money to bring his body home.

Alcoholism runs in families. All my friends' parents had cocktail parties and drank martinis before dinner, but Dad was more in the grip of alcohol than anyone realized. When I was eleven and away at summer camp, he took a bad fall on a timber-cruising trip and broke three vertebrae. His boss, Jack Starr, bundled him into the pickup truck and drove him forty miles over logging roads back to town. They got him into the community hospital and filled him full of morphine. He was in severe pain, and as the morphine and alcohol ebbed out of his system, he began to hallucinate.

The hospital called my mother, but the doctor wouldn't let her in to see him. "How much does your husband drink?" he barked at her. "Oh, you know, just ... well, he drinks, you know, I guess, like everybody," she said. She was scared to death, naturally, and thoroughly cowed by the brusque doctor. He gave her a look that assessed her I.Q. at about seventy. "Madam," he told her, "your husband is having the DTs, and my staff can't handle him. If you don't get somebody in here to mind him right quick, I am going to ship him up to the state hospital." My mother called someone Dad knew from one of his periodic visits to Alcoholics Anonymous. I am sure she cried. Within a few hours, AA members were keeping a twenty-four-hour vigil at Dad's bedside.

It was a long time before he came home. When my mother went to visit him, she'd have to leave us girls in the car because the hospital wouldn't allow us on the ward. "I'll tell Daddy to wave at you out the window," she'd tell us. Then she'd be gone. We'd wait for a long time, staring at a certain second-story window, watching the curtain flapping. Finally a white hand would emerge through the muslin, wave twice, and disappear.

Dad was an alcoholic in much the same way as his father had been, with the same periods of calm productivity, the same restless nights, the same inexplicable spasms of drunkenness. The one big difference was that Dad never got mean or violent when he drank, just weepy and maudlin. He would sit with a glass of gin in the living room, curtains drawn, lights off, smoking cigarettes and listening to mournful music on the hi-fi. His favorite was Grieg's gloomy Norwegian tone poem, *Peer Gynt*. Sometimes when he was in a melancholy mood he'd go down to the Elks Club and ask the piano player to play "Åse's Death" from *Peer Gynt*. "Åse's Death" is the mother of all funeral dirges. If there weren't too many patrons left, the piano player would indulge him. "That song is a real bar-cleaner," said my dad.

When he was sober, my dad helped me with my long division—turned out he wasn't very good at it either. He took us girls with him, together or separately, when he went to see his business friends. Sometimes I'd get to go on board a Japanese ship with him, but more often I hung around on the dock and watched the ships rise and fall at their moorings, watched the brisk, uniformed sailors walking the decks. I would put my face down close to the cracks between the dock timbers and watch the water, dark with engine oil and bearing grease and flecked with bobbing splinters and chunks of bark. I would smell the vast sawdust piles, and draw into my lungs that thin resinous odor, sweet as gin on a man's breath.

We moved from the duplex into a big, old, falling-down house nearer the center of town. I started the seventh grade at Marshfield Junior High School, and Mom taught at the high school. As the oldest, it was my job to see my sisters off to school and lock the door. Dad's habits were unpredictable—sometimes he was there in the morning; sometimes he wasn't; sometimes he was there but unable to take anything in. I always locked up, sometimes leaving him sleeping on the couch.

One evening after I'd finished the dishes and was headed upstairs to my room, my mother pulled me aside and told me, in a low, even voice, "I filed for divorce today. I thought you should know." I looked at her to discern whether an answer was required. None seemed to be. I nodded and turned to go to my room.

A few days after that Daddy left for California. There was a job for him at the truck dealership where Uncle Ken worked. He didn't know how long he'd be gone. He knew I would help my mother; she wasn't having an easy time. His earnest blue eyes, puffy around the edges, probed me and pinned me to my chair as I ate my oatmeal. I could tell his heart was breaking.

Soon after that we moved to California to join him, and the marriage held together for a couple more years. After the divorce, Mom took us girls and moved to Washington and then back to Oregon, into Grandma and Grandpa's old house on Elkins Road. All that took a few years, during which Dad bounced around California and Oregon and finally landed near Molalla.

He would come over and do little chores for her. He built a bed for my sister Leslie in the little basement bedroom, the one Gavin later lived in as a boy, the room where I'm now writing this story. He paneled the basement wall with cedar shakes, giving it a cozy, elvish feel, like a burrow. Sometimes, when he was working, he'd come and take us all out to dinner. These were wonderful times. We were a family again and none of the bad things had happened. Once we went to a snooty restaurant, and Dad ordered prime rib. He was sober and in fine form, joking and laughing, and he and Mom were teasing each other the way they did in the old days.

The waiter wheeled in a whole roast of beef on a trolley with a fancy silver lid. He opened it and picked up the carving knife. Dad looked at the silver lid and then at the waiter. Behind his hand and not quite softly enough, he murmured, "Looks like a coffin for a midget." The waiter's lips tightened.

"Oh, Daddy," we said. "Be serious!" We were proud of him for being sober and witty and with us.

"Oh, I am," he said. "I'm always serious when I'm eating midgets."

This was before he got sick from the throat cancer. He was living with a vigorous Swedish lady named Beulah, who scolded him, coddled him, and took care of him. She had an old, plain, comfortable house next to the Molalla River. I would visit and spend the night and listen to the river flowing over the stones. After a few years Beulah despaired of sobering him up, and she kicked him out. He moved in with Uncle Shafer on his little farm near Oregon City. He was pretty sick by this time. He lived in Shafer's back garden in a trailer he'd built himself. There was no place to sit inside, so I would usually take him for a ride in my car, my babies in the backseat, looking for a coffee shop or a hamburger place. Sometimes Dad could lead us right to a good restaurant. Sometimes all he remembered were the bars. "I can't take the kids in there, Daddy," I said.

"Let me tell you one thing," Dad said on one of these visits. "Never be sick and poor at the same time."

By many people's lights, when he died at sixty-four, he died a failure. A cliché you hear about alcoholics is "A good person with a bad disease." That doesn't exactly match my dad. "Good" is too simple and sweet. He was complicated. I guess the reason I'm telling this story at all is that I don't want to leave the impression that he was nothing but an alcoholic, or that his alcoholism was the most important thing about him. Alcoholism so overwhelms a person, a family, that it's tempting sometimes to make it your whole identity. Dad didn't do that. He wore the disease like a mask, a garment; it did not explain everything about him; it just covered up parts of him that he didn't want to reveal. He suffered more pain in his life, physical and mental, than most people suffer. The alcohol was an anesthetic that dulled the pain and made it possible for him to get through the day. But so did his wacky jokes and his love of wordplay; these were the milder analgesics that helped him laugh. He made us laugh. He called potatoes "po-nine-toes"—"because of the inflation these days, you know." Once I explained, earnestly, "But, Daddy, you really should say, 'pot-NINE-oes', so it matches 'pot-EIGHT-oes." He gave me a tender smile, but he still said "po-NINE-toes."

He called me "Lizzie" when he was in a good mood. He liked to say, "Lizzie, your old dad has a left-handed sense of humor." He had an eighth-grade education and a GED, yet he loved to read the essays of Anatole France and other such intellectuals. His love for us girls was extravagant, yet he had a touch of brutality that he could not always conceal. He once hurled the word "cripple" at my sister Melinda, whose odd childhood ways used to worry him and my mother. This was after she was an adult and it was clear she was never going to be right.

Dad had an inexplicable condition—alcoholism? life?—that baffled and maddened him, as it did all of us who loved him. He fought his demons and he lost. Or so it seems.

Yet I know his life had moments of happiness and joy, because I shared many of them. Before he got sick he was blessed with longer periods of sobriety, weeks and months when he was free from the grip of addiction. These were wonderful while they lasted. He was able to enjoy moments of simple sweetness: smoking a cigarette and watching the sun go down and listening to the crickets, petting his dog Snoose, eating fresh tomatoes from Beulah's garden. Visiting him with Gavin and Mary helped me know my father again the way I remembered him when I was a little girl. Dad would take Gavin on his lap and tell him the stories he used to tell me, stories about Hodags, fabulous beasts, half mountain goat and half something else (I forget), whose right legs were shorter than their left legs so they could walk even-keeled around the mountain.

He was proud of his accomplishments. "Your old dad knows a *little* something about logs and lumber," he used to say. He was proud of his children. "Lizzie," he would say to me again and again, "did I ever tell you I love you?"

Coming Home

My aunt Eunice, my dad's youngest sister, called me in August to say she would be traveling up from California over Labor Day weekend, and why didn't I throw a family party for her? I was not surprised, not entirely pleased. Opening my home to my family seems to be the role I have slipped into, one I do not always embrace. It is one thing to invite your family in; it is another to be expected always to be available when the family wants to come home.

The role came with the position of eldest daughter, and it came even more strongly with the house, as I knew it would. Even though this aged house along the Little Lucky came to John and me from my mother's Thompson side, my father's Peterson relatives regard our home as something that belongs to them, too. After all, Mom and Dad were married here, and they stayed married for sixteen years, and though their love was battered and pulled askew, it persisted in both of them even after they were divorced. "Virginia?" Dad would call out when he needed her, momentarily forgetting he was now living with Eileen, or Beulah. "Your dad used to be quite a dancer," Mom would tell me in one of her rare nostalgic moods, remembering the dances at the Runeberg Hall in Coos Bay, when they put us babies down to sleep on piles of coats in the corner and lilted each other around the floor to the strains of a Swedish hambo on the accordion in slow three-quarter time. Mom and Daddy were poignantly tender with each other until he died in 1984. Daddy's relatives, like Mom's, feel the pull of home in this place.

When Eunice asked me to have the party, my life was overfull. I had a new job. Gavin and Mary were old enough to have a social life but too young to drive. And then there were the unending homeplace chores. I agreed to do it, but would she please issue the invitations? She said she would invite everybody except her nephew, my cousin David. There is bad blood between them stemming from the time David handled the sale of her brother Ken's fishing boat. "What he did was absolutely inexcusable," she says. I don't know what he did and I don't want to know. I barely know David, who's a whole generation older than me. I told Eunice I wasn't getting into the middle of any family fights. If I was having the party, everybody would get an invitation.

"I simply couldn't face David if he were there," she said, her tone suddenly chilly. "Maybe I just won't come." That is your prerogative, I told her, hoping I sounded a little bit snotty but not too much. Then she relented and said I could invite him if I wished, but she absolutely wouldn't, because they weren't speaking.

Well, as I said, things were busy, and I was expecting the word to go through the family grapevine, and so the party slipped out of my immediate attention. The short of it is, I didn't get hold of David until it was too late. I had been hoping he would hear about it from his brother Tim, but Eunice was slow getting started on the invitations, and then Tim was out of town when she did send word, and so David didn't get the news until a few days before Labor Day.

I called David on Thursday night. "If we'd known about it sooner, we'd have been glad to come," he told me reproachfully. I stammered excuses, the workload, the kids … I said I'd asked Eunice to issue the invitations, and … "Oh, yes. My dear Aunt Eunice," said David in poisoned tones.

This is not my business! I thought. Why didn't I just refuse to have the party? Why didn't I insist that Eunice invite David? But it was too late. I swore and ground my teeth. Nobody could make a home for this impossible family.

A writing-teacher friend of mine told me she asks her students to write about how they know when they are home. Hearing this, I think of all the clichés I've heard about home. Home is where the heart is. (Whatever can that mean?) Home is the place where, if you have to go there, they have to take you in. When

John and I moved here twenty years ago, this house, this ruined old schoolhouse that Grandpa had turned into a plain, quirky dwelling, was the closest thing I knew to a family home. It was the one constant of place among the many places my family occupied when I was a child.

It was surely my memories of golden wheat and ripening filberts and the sun setting over the purple Coast Range that made this place seem like Eden from the vantage point of a small Seattle apartment. Which of course was a home; it had a roof and walls and a kitchen. And we were happy. John was going to college and I was raising two babies. We were lucky to live in a decent place.

But it didn't feel like home. It felt like a temporary billet between an unstable past and an unformed future. When Mom offered to sell us this house cheap, we accepted joyfully. What we knew and didn't want to know was that it was a wreck, with a leaky roof and peeling paint and rattly windows and sloping floors and a basement that filled with water every winter. None of that mattered. We were homeless, and now we were going home.

August had been warm, but I'd kept up with the watering, and the yard looked good. I even watered the lawn, something I don't usually bother with. I put the kids to work washing windows and knocking cobwebs down with the broom. I bought some new lawn chairs, and I scrubbed the wooden porch swing. I asked some friends to come and play their guitars.

John cooked hamburgers on the grill, and I made ice cream in the electric freezer. The aunts and cousins laid out potato salad and coleslaw. Cousin Shirley brought marinated broccoli with bacon, and cousin Sharon brought her famous Cool Whip Ambrosia, a pink froth of fruit cocktail and maraschino cherries and artificial whipped cream. Everyone was there except Uncle Ken, a reluctant traveler, and David. I don't think David holds it against me. He knows Eunice very well.

We sat outside in the thin September sunshine. Eunice held court in a lawn chair, telling us how she had given her brother

Ken a home after a series of life blows had left him more or less permanently without resources. Uncle Ken is my father's next-older brother. He's never had a big drinking problem, but he sometimes forgets to take care of himself. He takes care of other people instead. When Dad and Ken were in their twenties and their mother got sick with cancer, Ken got a job on a fishing boat in Alaska and sent his whole paycheck home every month. Many years later, when he was one step above living on the street—as Eunice tells it—she took him in. "I knew he'd drive me crazy," she said, "but after he took care of my mother, I figured he had it coming."

For the past twenty-five years Uncle Ken has lived with Eunice in a little room in her garage. He putters constantly, keeping her yard up in his own fashion, pointedly not following her directions. When I visited Eunice a few years ago, she waved her hand over the backyard and groaned. "I told Ken to stomp down those horse turds he put on the flower beds," she said. "And there they are, big as apples."

He drives her crazy. Sitting in her lawn chair, she said, "I tell him over and over, DON'T TOUCH my roses; let me take care of them," she said. "Then he goes and prunes them right down to the ground because somebody at the hardware store told him that's how you prune roses." She lifted her hands to heaven.

"Well, Eunice," said my cousin Tim. "You say you tell him over and over. Has it ever done any good?" Everybody laughed except Eunice, who looked puzzled. "No," she said. "I don't understand it. I've often thought he must have attention-deficit disorder."

An elderly brother and sister making a home together, loving each other, driving each other crazy. The love must be stronger than the craziness, or else one of them, or both, would be dead by now. Or homeless.

I remember the time when my father was particularly down on his luck and asked if he could come live with John and me. It was a couple of years after we'd moved here. John was going to computer school and I was staying home with our children. Gavin was six, Mary was three. We were scraping by, and the house was in tough shape.

"It'd be for a couple of weeks, a month maybe, till I get on my feet," said my father.

Through the telephone I parsed his words, his tone of voice, wondering where he was. He sounded sober, but for how long? I remembered the bad years before the divorce, how he would come and go randomly, inexplicably. Sometimes he was home but unable to fathom what you wanted of him. Sometimes he was heartbreakingly lucid.

"Daddy," I said, "We have no place to put you."

"Oh. All right."

"I'm sorry, Daddy, I'm sorry," I told him.

"That's all right, honey," he said. "You can't hurt me. I've been dumped on by the experts."

I wonder if most people in my family have been, at one time or another, homeless, if not in fact, then in heart. I know I have moments when my heart goes traveling somewhere far from home, and then it doesn't matter how comfortable it is where my body lives.

But eventually I come home, and the home I come to is this old schoolhouse on Elkins Road, rehabilitated by the vigorous carpentry of my grandfather and gradually redeemed, corner by corner and board by board, by John and me, by our muscle and sweat, by our living and enduring and loving and hating this place into a state of grace.

Detritus

≋≋≋

Elkins Road is a road that invites walks. It's a country road, a two-lane macadam with no center stripe except around the corners. It takes off from Old Highway 99 at the foot of a little rise, cuts through the hilltop, and then winds down into the narrow valley of the Little Lucky, a rolling landscape of grass-seed fields and Christmas tree plantations. On the western horizon is the Coast Range, folded purple hills fading backward from dark to pale as the sun goes down.

It's a pretty road, a pretty valley. When people come to visit us for the first time, they always exclaim about that little rise, how the road lifts them gently and lowers them into the valley, how the valley spreads itself out like a green feast. Some of them, the ones who live in Portland or Seattle, say, "You're so lucky to be out here, away from all the people."

I tell them truthfully that I never get tired of being here along this road. I like walking it better than driving it. There is always something interesting to see that can't be experienced fully from a car window—the gray bull in the field next to ours (I've never seen another one that color), the pheasant I occasionally flush from the roadside bushes, the redwing blackbirds sitting on the power wires crying, "Pumpkin-eater!" These are the things that make my city friends tell me how lucky I am.

But they're wrong about there being no people here. This valley has been inhabited for a long, long time, ten thousand years or more. The Kalapuya people lived along the Big Lucky and all over the Willamette Valley. The name Luckiamute came from them. It must have been a lush land, a paradise of game, fish, wild grains, nuts, berries, and camas root. You wouldn't know they'd been here just by looking, because the Kalapuya didn't leave much trace of their daily lives. I think of them when I see camas flowering in the ditches on Mother's Day.

My own ancestors, in contrast, wrote their stories all over the landscape, and so do we today. You can read our big stories in the farm fields and drainage ditches, in the roads and cities, the dams and clear-cuts, the power lines and green lawns. You can read the smaller ones in the trash by the roadside, the crumpled ephemera of people's lives lying abandoned in the ditches. I'm speaking of the dreary parade of Coors cans, Bud bottles, Big Mac boxes, potato-chip bags, motor-oil containers, paper diapers, flattened six-pack cartons, crushed cigarette wrappers—the familiar trickle of plastic, tinfoil, Mylar, waxed paper, pasteboard, Styrofoam, and waterlogged French fries that lines my road on both sides, the midden heaps of twenty-first-century culture.

All these things make me piece together stories. Some have more narrative promise than others. The other day I found a plastic egg tray from the inside of a refrigerator door, ripped whole and jagged-edged from the smooth molded panel. The sight of this egg tray, upside-down and almost in the ditch, raises questions for me. Why would somebody rip an egg tray out of the inside of a refrigerator in the first place? And then why discard it right there? Is the rest of the refrigerator there somewhere, too—buried out beyond the barbed-wire fence, maybe? Did some appliance mover go berserk one day, erupting in a rage of mayhem and dismemberment, scattering refrigerator parts across six counties? Will some other innocent walker, maybe a century from now, find a crisper drawer? A little hinged door marked, "Butter"?

Once I found a plastic photo frame with a waterlogged snapshot still in it. The picture showed a smiling dark-haired woman sitting on a man's lap in a dark living room. The man's arms were around the woman's waist, and his face was obscured by her shoulders. Was this photo once on top of a piano, or a bedside table? Was it lost in a move, perhaps, fallen from a pickup truck heaped with the woman's belongings? Does she miss it, grieve for it even now? Or was it flung in rage or disgust from a cranked-down car window? Does she remember that happy time in the picture? Does he?

Another time I found a tract called "The Way," published, it said inside, by the Church of God of Prophecy. Across the top was written, in what I imagine to be a teenager's round hand, the name "Shawna Vaugn." Why should Shawna Vaugn want to put her name on something so ephemeral as a religious tract? (And does she really spell it "Vaugn"?) Does it mean young Shawna (if she is young) is very devout, or is she merely possessive of her things? If she is devout (or possessive), how could she just throw the tract away? Maybe it slipped from her purse as she waited for the school bus. Or maybe Shawna Vaugn isn't devout at all. Maybe she has a friend who's trying to convert her, and this friend chose the tract for Shawna and thoughtfully wrote her name across the top (misspelling it), and then lost the tract on the way to Shawna's house. Was this friend embarrassed to arrive empty-handed? Or was it supposed to be a surprise, and if so did she invent some other reason for her visit? Did she get another tract for Shawna? Did Shawna want it? Did Shawna fling it out of the car the first chance she got?

On that same walk I found a man's rubber-soled canvas shoe, size eleven. Forty feet down the road was the other shoe. They were not sneakers, but canvas Oxfords, the kind of shoes you might see on a neat old man wearing a white linen shirt with pintucks down the bosom and square-cropped tails hanging outside the waistband of his trousers. The shoes were soggy and dirty but not worn out. How could this man throw away a perfectly good pair of shoes? And why first one and then the other? Did he slow the car and remove his shoes and throw them, one at a time, out the window? Did he drive home in his stocking feet? Did somebody else in the car—a lady friend, perhaps—snatch his shoes away and wave them out the window, laughing, and then carelessly let go? Was it too dark to go back and find them? Or were they too merry or too drunk or too mad at each other?

My favorite walk is westward from my house, up the gravel road to the top of the ridge. From there you can see the Coast Range up close, with the western part of the valley spread out at its feet. The last time I walked up there I found, in an uncultivated finger of field alongside the road, a new artifact. It was a fresh grave, about five feet by three, ringed by stones and marked with a wooden cross about four feet high. The cross was made of fir two-by-fours, unvarnished but carefully planed and sanded smooth. The center joint was a mortise-and-tenon, fastened together with dowel pegs sanded flush with the surface.

Someone had clearly taken pains with this cross, and he (she?) had done a beautiful job. But who, and why? There was no inscription on the cross or anywhere on the grave. The mound, too small to cover a human coffin, was probably the grave of a dog, I decided, a favorite hunting dog or house pet, a member of the family for many years. Or maybe the dog was sole faithful companion of one lonely man, a man so grief-stricken at the death of his friend that he spent a rainy afternoon hunched over his table saw and his joiner. A man moved to write himself and his devotion on the landscape.

Puttering

꿈꿈

It's rare for me to be alone on a Saturday morning, but on this Saturday Gavin was collecting bottles with his Cub Scout pack and Mary had spent the night with a friend from her second-grade class. John was pruning apple trees. From the kitchen window I could see him across the orchard, bulky in his overalls and a gray sweatshirt, neck craned, face to the rain, maneuvering the twelve-foot pruning pole amid a thicket of gnarled branches.

I wandered out the front door and looked at the bare patch of ground next to the porch where, last October, John had dug a drainage trench along the foundation wall. His hard labor paid off—the basement stayed dry all winter—but now the soil looked naked and pitiful, clumpy with tangled roots and glistening clods. *Ferns,* I thought; *that's what it needs.* I hunted up the bicycle pump and pumped up the wheelbarrow tire. Then I fetched the spade and wheeled down into the woods.

Under the tallest pines is a massive colony of sword ferns, so thick it's hard to walk through. I eyed a smallish clump and stuck the spade in near where its edge seemed to be. The spade made sucking noises as I worked it around the rootball. In early March our Willamette Valley mud has a snot-slick quality that makes you skid across the garden in rubber boots. Stick a spade straight down and it thrums like a tuning fork. Dig, and you turn up slabs of clay dense as bricks, with shiny shovel-surfaces sweating drops of water. The ground seems yielding, but its softness covers a fierce resistance.

Finally, grunting and panting, I levered the clump out of the ground and carried it to the wheelbarrow, stumbling a bit over the rough ground. I went back and wiggled out a couple more clumps and headed for the house.

On the way I passed the vegetable garden, comatose under its winter mulch of black plastic. *Surely there's something I can plant,* I thought. I heeled in the ferns without much ceremony—

it's hard to hurt them. Then I went into the house and rooted through the deep freeze, where I found last year's seeds, peas and lettuce and turnips. From the kitchen I took a paring knife.

Back at the vegetable garden, I cut Xs in the plastic and poked the seeds down into the mud with my fingers, pushing in the holes with the heel of my hand. From time to time I stood up to survey the rest of the garden, thinking ahead to tomatoes, peppers, eggplant, cantaloupe. Where should they go? *Pretty soon I'll need to flush out the irrigation drippers. Maybe we'll try watermelons this year. Or okra. I'd like to try cooking a real gumbo some time.*

I had a few lettuce seeds left over, so I dribbled them into the pots out on the patio. The pots had been sitting there since last year's geraniums died. I scrabbled the soil with my fingers and laid the seeds in among the vermiculite pellets. Fussing with the geranium pots got me thinking about the perennial bed out front. I wheeled the wheelbarrow over there and, squatting on my heels, scraped away the rotted blackness from last summer's garden. With soaked, stained gloves I pulled bittercress and chickweed and quackgrass up by the muddy roots. As I worked I dreamed of the baby's breath and black-eyed Susans, the Shirley poppies and salvia that would soon push their way out of the moist earth.

Already the silvery feathers of California poppies had emerged, and the columbines, with their leaves all crinkly like a new baby's wet hair. A calla lily was unfurling its first frond next to the crabapple tree. Already blooming under the Japanese maple were three primroses, survivors from the five I'd put in last spring.

The crabapple and the Japanese maple needed pruning, so I fetched the clippers from the greenhouse. The crabapple is just next to where the ivy-covered front bank slopes down to the road. *Soon I'll put a photinia hedge along there*, I said to myself. Just take a mattock and scalp off the ivy and get a dozen plants and pop them in. And then I would get to work on the red climbing roses at the other end. A trellis: how could we build one cheap? Maybe use apple prunings? Then I would put in fragrant bush roses, buxom sprawls of Maiden's Blush and Madame Pierre Oger amid lavender and borage, all sweetness and spice and honeybees buzzing in the sun.

Puttering and dreaming. With shears still in hand I stood next to the crabapple, thinking for a minute. Then I headed around back to the blueberries and clipped them into shape, pausing for a moment to stick the crabapple prunings into a patch of garden dirt; *maybe they'll take root for me.* As I worked I surveyed the fallow rectangle next to the blueberries. What to put in there? *Rhubarb? Asparagus? There's room for both ...*

About one o'clock there came a rain squall and I saw John heading for the house. I went inside to make coffee. I ate a sandwich and looked at garden magazines. All the gardens in them are so planned, so perfect, so regular in their tidy irregularity. It used to intimidate me, reading these magazines. I used to draw circles on graph paper and mark them "Hellebore," "Candytuft." But now I don't buy that vision of expensive perfection. When I read about some suburban couple who "create" a garden with a landscape architect and store-bought plants, I raise my head and look at my mother's billowing peonies, the yellow iris I got from my friend Kathy, the rhubarb Steve dug for us from his garden. I like my garden in all its unplanned randomness.

It isn't unplanned, exactly. I plan it by dreaming as I putter. The dreams take shape in my head when my hands are busy pruning or weeding or planting. I just follow the lead of the tasks, the shape of the weather, the lay of the land. Attend to what catches the eye, do what comes to hand, and let my imagination ramble as a bee rambles from one blossom to the next, with no map, no itinerary, just doing the next thing.

Manure, I mused as I set down my empty coffee cup. Last fall I should have dug some manure into the asparagus bed. There's still time.

Melinda

My sister met me at the door of the YWCA, wearing a sweatshirt with a yellow and orange cartoon cat on it and a pair of baggy blue doubleknit pants. Her hair was mussed on top, but clean. She gave me a broad smile, kind of rocking on her feet as she approached me. She walks with a rolling gait, like a sailor just off the boat.

"Do I look good?" she asked, hugging me and then stepping back, letting me have a look at her. As always, I said, "You look great, Melinda."

"Everybody says I don't look thirty-eight."

"That's right," I said. "You look young for your age." She smiled; she expected this. "I buy my own food, you know. I make good coffee."

My sister lives on the third floor of the YWCA. She carries her room key in her right hand and a Kleenex in her left, everywhere she goes. The Kleenex is to stanch her chronic nosebleeds, which she's had ever since she was a little girl. The population at the Y tends to be a transient bunch. Melinda has lived here longer than anybody, ever since a woman was murdered at the low-income apartment house where she lived before. That was a time when she was afraid to wash her hair because the water might turn to blood.

"I'll show you what I bought," she said, handing me a floppy stuffed bunny. "It's a stuffed animal," she said, grinning. Awkwardly, I took the bunny and handed her the package. She tore it open, didn't read the card, seized the check. "Oh, thank you!" she said at the picture, John and me and the kids, taken last Christmas. She seemed really pleased, and suddenly my heart surged. "Do I look thirty-eight?" she demanded. "Everybody says I don't look thirty-eight."

"No," I said. "You don't." She really doesn't. Although the medication makes the corners of her mouth twitch when she speaks, her face is unlined and fresh, and her eyes are as bright as they were when she was a little girl.

I sat carefully in the chair closest to the door, a rumpsprung rocker. Her eight-by-twelve cubicle is crammed with stuff. The closet doors were open, as always, and the contents—pants, shirts, robes, shoes, underwear, gleaned from the Goodwill, the charity boxes, and the dumpster—spilled out into the room. Her bed and desk took up about half the floor space, and a T.V. tray, two chairs, a laundry basket, and a stuffed duffel bag filled most of the rest. Spring dampness came in through the open window, mingling with the rumblings of motorcycles and the smell of dirty laundry.

On a shelf above Melinda's bed were a Bible, a Book of Mormon, the Mormon Doctrine and Covenants, the Pearl of Great Price, and a new book, The Christian Mother Goose. I flipped through it while she fixed the coffee. "Mistress Mary, quite contrary, how does your garden grow? God sends the sun and God sends the rain, and the flowers bloom all in a row." And this verse, Bowdlerized into gentleness: "Rock-a-bye baby, on the tree top. When the wind blows, the cradle will rock. Mother will knit the baby a shawl, and God will bless Mother, Baby, and all." I wish it were that way, I thought.

Melinda said, "They gave me this coffee for my birthday. It was my birthday, and they gave me this coffee."

"Do you mean the people down at the Beanery?"

"Yeah. It was my birthday, and they gave it to me." Melinda is one of "the coffee people," as a waitress friend of mine calls them, the untethered ones who nurse a coffee and a refill over a long, ruminating afternoon. The restaurants give Melinda credit, and she is faithful about paying them back from her four hundred twenty dollars a month. Often they'll slip her a cup of coffee or a cookie for free.

"Edith thinks my coffee is too strong," she said, as the coffee began to drip. "She doesn't like my coffee."

"Edith?"

"Yeah. She says my coffee is too strong. She says, 'Melinda, you make it too strong.'" She mimicked a high, prissy voice.

I wondered who Edith is or was, wondered whether this happened yesterday or twenty years ago.

"She's a bitch," said Melinda cheerfully. "But I put up with it because she's the manager."

There was a time when her mind would find a groove and play it again and again. "You don't know what it's like in the hospital," she'd say, over and over, and no attempt at ordinary conversation would deter her. "You don't know what it's like in the hospital. You don't know what it's like." Today the flashes and short circuits of her brain carry her over a wider mental landscape, and I fall behind when I try to follow.

"My church friends came to see me today." Melinda converted to the Mormon faith after missionaries came upon her at the Y and supplied her with food and clothing and attention and invitations to church. She observes all the teachings of the church except the one about not drinking coffee. She has been forthright with the elders about this, and the result, she says, is that she will not be allowed into the Temple. She shrugs; she'd rather have her coffee.

We sipped in silence for a moment. "Bob told me in the swimming pool that I was his enemy. I don't want to marry someone like that."

"Bob?"

"Yeah. He told me I was his enemy. In the swimming pool."

"And you don't want to marry him."

"No. Would you?"

"No, I guess not," I admitted. "Did he want you to marry him?"

"Yeah."

"Ah." She makes me nervous. I'm edgy, awkward, wary of what might be behind the bushes in this foreign schizophrenic landscape.

I shifted around in the rocker, trying to avoid the probing springs.

"Do you want me to play my accordion for you?"

"Sure." She pulled it out, slung her arms through the straps, and began a gospel tune, starting slow and accelerating until her fingers are flying. Her bright eyes went flat, staring nowhere.

She played like an automaton, a player piano, hitting most of the melody keys and the oom-pa-pa buttons but with absolutely flat dynamics and phrasing.

When she was little, four or five, she could hear a tune once or twice and pick it out on the piano. She sang a sweet soprano when the four of us girls made harmony in the car on long trips. In the years when she was getting sick and nobody knew what was the matter with her, she'd play the piano for hours, "Für Elise" over and over, banging it out, her mind a needle scratching the groove, scratching the groove. That was a time when she broke Mom's finger because she saw snakes where Mom's hair should have been.

There were signs all through her childhood, but it took our parents a while to piece them together. She was a long time learning to walk, to talk. Her schoolwork was spotty; she did well in reading and writing, but in math she brought home zeroes. That's not so uncommon, and it's not crazy, but once she brought home a math paper on which she'd written, over and over: "I can't do it! Ha Ha Ha! I can't do it! Ha Ha Ha!"

Her disease emerged full-blown when she was seventeen. She lived in this house on the Little Lucky with our mother and two younger sisters, Laurie and Leslie. I was away at college and no help to anybody. Mom, who had gotten her master's in social work a couple of years earlier, was a case worker for the state welfare office in Salem. She was at work one afternoon when Leslie called: "Mom, you'd better come home right away. Melinda is down on all fours and barking like a dog." By the time Mom got home, Melinda was in tears, terrified of what she had become. "Oh, Mom," she sobbed as my mother held her close and tried to soothe her. "Oh, Mom, I wish I was somebody else!"

In those days, the figure of "the schizophrenogenic mother," who was thought to cause the child's schizophrenia, dominated psychiatric theory. My mother sought help from a psychiatrist, who told her Melinda's condition was all her fault. She must have believed it herself. She took Melinda to the state psychiatric hospital in Salem. The doctor forbade them to have any contact beyond my mother's regular visits. The hospital had a resident high-school program for teenage schizophrenics. With medication, Melinda got well enough to resume her studies, and she graduated while she was still in the hospital.

Now, two decades later and with the help of her medication, she has gotten to the place where she can live more or less independently at the Y. Here she is safe, and her mind is free to range through the past, visiting old haunts, looking up old friends, bumbling from one encounter to another like a bee among flowers. My mooring to the straightness of things keeps me from joining her, but I can sometimes follow her rambles from where I sit, anchored in the rocking chair, smelling the dirty socks.

She looked up as she finished the hymn. "Do you like it?" she asked. "Do you think I'm a good accordion player?" Yes, I assured her, yes. "What's that song?" I ask this every time. She shrugged, not much interested. "I don't know any of them," she said. "I just play 'em."

And then she's off into the next one, a polka, playing at a machine-gun tempo. I rock and pat my foot, suspended outside time as the polka chatters and yammers its course. My body sags in the low-bottomed chair, and I am enveloped in music, saturated with music, drowning in it. I don't know how, but peace invades my bones. I rock and pat my foot.

The third tune was familiar, and I hummed along. It was another gospel song, an old one I've always liked, and I sang snatches of the words softly as they came to me. "Why should I feel discouraged? Why should the shadows come?" She played on, paying no attention. "For His eye is on the sparrow." I felt lightheaded and a little teary.

"Do you know that one?" I asked as she finished. She shook her head, frowning, concentrating on God knows what inside her brain. I told her the name of the song, but she wasn't listening. She put the accordion away, and I knew it was time to go.

"I don't look thirty-eight, do I?" she said at the door.

"No," I said, smiling. "You don't look thirty-eight."

Gathering Wood

≈≈

We got going early Sunday morning, John and I, knowing we had only a few hours. John began building a lean-to against the chicken house with poles he'd cut from our woodlot. I set to work with wheelbarrow and leather gloves and a machete.

Because we both work at regular jobs, the chores have to be fitted into odds and ends of time, packed in around track meets and softball games and choir practice and late nights at the office. It's hard to do anything systematically or with sustained effort. A Sunday in late September was none too soon to get started with the firewood, but there was no help for it. My task was to gather the untidy piles of wood that John had cut the past couple of years. After a season or two the piles get covered with blackberry vines so thick you can't even see the wood underneath.

One of these piles was underneath the Jona-Red apple tree. The ground was carpeted with a soft red rottenness that sent forth a pungent smell. The apples rolled and slipped under my feet as I whacked away with the machete and heaved chunks of wood at the wheelbarrow. I had to step carefully, but even so I couldn't help disturbing the yellowjackets gorging themselves on the soft flesh. They retreated sluggishly, too satiated to sting.

I remembered when we first came here, how I swept those apples into cider, applesauce, and jelly like a fanatical housewife sweeping a kitchen clean. I'd send the kids out to scour the ground of windfalls, and I'd lug five-gallon buckets full of them up to the back porch. I wasted nothing. This place was to be our homestead, our cabin on the frontier. We would live off the land by the sweat of our brows. We would grow beans and tomatoes and can them for winter. I would grind my own flour and sew my children's clothes.

I didn't talk much about this then, because it sounded corny. I talked instead about the favorable terms, the low interest rate, the wisdom of buying a house just now. When a couple of friends told me that they admired us for going "back to the land," as if The Land were some place we had all been kicked out of, I felt embarrassed. Well, that's not it really, I told them, and most of the time I believed that. But a vision of snug independence obsessed me on a wordless level. That vision seemed to offer a promise of freedom, or maybe it was redemption. I knew it came at a price, a justification by works that I thought I was prepared for.

Two wheelbarrow loads, three. John's lean-to was taking shape, a foursquare structure with a peaked roof. The poles were knobby and slightly bent, but the framework looked supple and strong, like a Swiss Family Robinson treehouse. It was hot, and John had tied a blue bandanna around his head. As I rolled in with another load of wood, he looked at me with his blue eyes and grinned, and sang, "Oh, life on the farm is kinda laid back ..."

Four wheelbarrow loads, six. At the other end of the pile was a prune tree, a Brooks variety, small and heavy with bruise-colored fruit. For the first few years we took good care of the fruit trees, especially the apples. I pruned them yearly, standing on a rickety picking ladder for hours in chilly January, lopping and sawing until my arms ached. The trees rewarded us with applesauce, cider, and dried apples to last through the winter, all of course at the cost of many more hours of labor.

This year I've hardly looked at the orchard. I've hardly walked out the back door. We didn't even plant a vegetable garden. As I duck under the apple branches with another armload of punky wood, a whippety limb smacks me in the face, and I'm hearing an old mental refrain: What's the matter with me that I can't take care of things around here? That I can't (choose one—hell, choose all of them): prune the apples, mow the orchard, clear the brush, cut back the peonies, divide the irises, weed the strawberries, thatch the lawn, water the compost pile, reglaze the greenhouse .... For a moment I'm back in a familiar slough of guilt. I cleanse myself with a wave of anger, and the anger too is for me—for letting myself slide into that slough, for failing to master the mental discipline of tolerating imperfect surroundings. For living too long in that state of can't-change-it-and-can't-stand-it.

Season by season, year by year, this place is beating the perfectionism out of me. But it isn't gone yet, not by a long stretch. At moments like these, I am stunned by the clarity of the fact that we are never going whip this place into shape. I ask myself, *What are we doing out here, anyway?* What in God's name were we thinking? What are we trying to prove? John drives sixty miles to work; I drive twenty, in the opposite direction. School is a twelve-mile round trip for the kids. Our weekdays are as harried as any family's anywhere, with school conferences, games, meets, youth group. Afternoons at work stretching into evenings, days when all I can do is dash home, throw something on the table for supper, and collapse into bed.

And on weekends here we are, pretending to be Jeffersonian small farmers. Jefferson, I remind myself sourly, had slaves. Why don't we quit kidding ourselves?

Later in the afternoon I showered, smoothed lotion on my sticker-scratched arms, and drove Mary into town to visit her friend Jasmine. After I dropped her off I prowled through the development, looking at the cheery houses with their bay windows, their neat little lawns. What were we hanging onto so fiercely, out there on the Little Lucky? I used to have a faint contempt for such suburban sameness. I got it from my father, spoiled by his craftsmanship and his disdain for tract houses. "Listen to that!" Dad would say, slamming the front door on a model house that looked like every other house on the street. "You can hear the studs rattle!" Why was I now looking at these houses with something close to longing?

"I'm tired," I whispered, wheeling the car onto the highway. But on the drive home I put such thoughts out of my mind. It wasn't so bad. Yes, the place is a lot of work, but we knew that going into it. We're young and strong, with more muscle than money. We're earning our life. It's a good life. We're comfortable, mostly happy. And there are moments of pure rock-bottom joy, moments too sublime to have been bought and paid for with work.

As I turned onto Elkins Road and crested the rise, these moments dimpled the surface of my memory like trout rippling a mountain lake. Pushing a small boy high in a swing and hearing him laugh into the universe and seeing all the golden fields in the world out beyond his feet. Picking a tomato in August and eating it right there, leaning over so the hot juice drips on my bare toes. Walking westward in September at twilight and seeing streaks of crystal rain slanting into the purple hollows of the Coast Range. Curling up next to the woodstove on New Year's Day with a mug of hot cider and a cinnamon stick. This place has given me moments of deep comfort. Weighing them alongside the hours of labor and the sore muscles would be like comparing cobbles to gold dust. They are like the pinpoints of gold in the bottom of the pan; you swirl and swirl and everything else washes away and the gold remains, and you can't dump it out if you try.

A few days after John finished the woodshed, I got a call from friends. They're pressing apples. Would I like to bring some over and make cider? The Jona-Reds were gone, but the later ones, those with the crisp white flesh and the ruby skin daubed with gold—we think they're Winesaps—were just coming ripe. I lined the pickup bed with newspaper and filled it with apples, and I collected as many juice bottles with lids as I could find.

The cider press was an old one, a stout oak-and-iron machine with a hand crank and a flywheel. We hosed the apples down and threw them into the hopper whole, worms and all, and the drum's steel fingers tore them to shreds and dropped them into the basket underneath. We slid the basket forward, cranked the press down, and the sweet juice flowed between the runnels and down the spout into a pan on the ground. The juice was thick, musky, spicy with vinegar.

It only took a couple of hours to press the whole load. I drove home carefully, ten gallons of cider in glass jars rattling behind me as I rounded the curves. It was a warm day, but I was dreaming of December and rain, and a fire crackling in the stove, and hot cider and cinnamon sticks.

Performance

❧❧

At the Saturday afternoon dress rehearsal I stood in the church kitchen drinking coffee and talking with the other angel mothers. Mary put her head in the door, and the look on her face told me to come right now.

I followed her out into the parish hall and we found a quiet corner. She was really too old for this, Mary said in a low voice, fighting tears. She was embarrassed to be here. She had been lured into it by the promise of a solo, but even that was hardly enough to make up for the little kids who tore around, yelling, in their angel costumes and then went mute and blank onstage and had to be prompted in a loud whisper by the Sunday-school teachers crouching in front of the first pew.

"And the worst of it is I have to wear this!" She spread her arms to display a skimpy, sleeveless shift that somebody had stitched up out of a bedsheet years before. It had sagging gaps between the snaps down the front and a big three-cornered tear on the right hip. It was hideous.

Then she did cry. "I had a nice costume," she sobbed, "but Tiffany said it was hers, and she made such a scene about it that I just took it off and told her to take it. And now I have to wear this! I'm not going to do it. I'm quitting right now."

We talked. She calmed down. She didn't quit. She had the solo, after all, and Mrs. Hopkins had been working for months on this play. She didn't want to let Mrs. Hopkins down, even if it meant appearing before the whole congregation in a torn bedsheet. "I'm proud of you," I told her. "We can at least take it home and wash it and iron it and fix that tear."

The next afternoon we dropped Mary and the costume in the Sunday-school wing and found our seats in the sanctuary. Presently the organ started a soft elaboration on the tune, "It Came Upon the Midnight Clear." The angels drifted in from the parish hall and assembled themselves on risers in front of the baptismal font. The risers were set up to resemble, roughly, a tree, with its top brushing the bottom of the baptismal font curtain. Mary, being the tallest angel, stood on the top riser. The main action took place center front—Joseph and Mary, the shepherds, the Wise Men.

There were awkward moments. At one point a Wise Man swept out his arm and intoned, "What is that I see in yonder East?" and there was no answer for a long, long time. The Wise Man held his pose. The angels shuffled their feet. One angel made a V with his two fingers and held it up over his neighbor's head. The congregation sat motionless. Finally, the answer came: "It is the Star of which we have been told." We all breathed again.

Mary's solo came near the end. Her pure, high, unselfconscious voice, floating out over the tops of the angels' heads, brought a little moisture to my eyes. But I was laughing, too, because her head was obscured by the curtain around the baptismal font. All I could see was her chin going up and down.

Her costume wasn't the pitiful rag she'd had on the day before. It was an elegant vestment of stiff, creamy cotton, gathered at the waist and shirred at the shoulders so that the sleeves draped softly over a full skirt. She looked a lot better than Tiffany, I noted with unholy satisfaction.

"That was beautiful, honey!" I told Mary afterward, as we stood in the cookie line. "Your song was perfect. Where did you get the costume?"

"Mrs. Hopkins made it for me." Mrs. Hopkins had gone home Saturday afternoon and sewn a costume from scratch. It must have taken her hours. "See, she gave me this card, too." Mary handed me a Christmas card with a singing angel on the front. Inside Mrs. Hopkins had written, "Mary, God has given you a beautiful voice. Use it for His glory, and ask nothing in return."

Earlier that week John and Gavin had gone down into our muddy woods and come back with a small Douglas fir, scragglier than the commercial sheared kind, but we like our Christmas trees spare. They carried it between them up to the house and eased it through the front door, its trunk oozing fragrant sap. Then Mary and I took our pruning shears down next to the stream and gathered pine boughs and cones and branches of holly and camellia and made a swag for the front door. We set out the nativity scene, all the figures except the baby Jesus. We made spritz and pepparkakor cookies and gingerbread men with cinnamon red-hots for eyes.

The tree at John's parents' house in Seattle would be a purchased noble fir twenty-five feet tall, its top grazing the elegant vaulted ceiling. It would be swathed in tasteful white lights, not like our homegrown tree with its motley multicolored strands. I cast a longing glance at our tree as I unplugged the lights and prepared to lock the front door. It was fine with me that we'd stayed home till Christmas Eve, even though it would be a long, traffic-clogged drive to Seattle. I'd much rather have stayed home altogether, but there was family to consider, and the obligations of the season.

We arrived late in the evening and spent a fitful night on the Hide-a-Bed mattress. Christmas morning was as chaotic as ever. The video camera was everywhere, poking its shiny bubble of an eye at everything—the wrapping paper littering the floor, the toddler with her flushed cheeks, the uncles exclaiming as they held up socks and sweaters. The thing oppressed me. I was tired and cranky. But I didn't want to be recorded forever with a scowl or a blank look on my face, so I assumed an expression of pleasant alertness and kept it on all day, until my eyebrows ached.

Maybe it was the video camera that gave the day's events a stream-of-consciousness feel. Or maybe in my weariness I switched off my interpretive apparatus and just took everything in, like the camera, without discrimination, without narrative. Whatever it was, the day comes back to me now as a montage of loosely imposed impressions. The bourbon-laced eggnog sank in the bowl and was replenished, and sank and was replenished, over and over. The mothers and aunts visited in a desultory way, in moments and snatches. The kids tore open package after package, and we paid attention, more or less. Balls clicked on the pool table downstairs. A football game on the television snagged our passing attention. The toddler rode her new doll stroller into the living room and out, in and out, until the seat ripped loose. Somebody played the piano intermittently, moodily noodling the keys.

I would have kept Christmas quietly, selfishly, at home, with good coffee instead of eggnog and Handel instead of football. Instead, I rose to the occasion. I smiled, asked polite questions of the uncles, hugged the children, dried the dishes. Sometimes the performance is all there is.

Stillness

When I was a teenager, my grandfather would roam through the house, turning off TVs and radios and grumbling about how the Younger Generation had to have noise all the time. "What's wrong with silence?" he would growl, twisting the radio knob until it snapped emphatically off, and silence would follow, at least for a while.

He had every right to do this. It was his house, after all. He had allowed his middle daughter and her three teenaged girls to move in, a decision for which I am sure he had at least momentary regrets. Grandpa and Grandma had lived a sedate life here after Grandpa retired from the mathematics department at the college in Monmouth. While Grandma sewed or worked in the yard, my grandfather pursued a quiet passion for genealogy, studying his books and papers through his swivel-armed magnifying glass, speaking on the telephone to friends, going into town twice or three times a week. He was at work on a family history, having traced his ancestry back to pre-colonial times in Boston and discovered that Thompson's Island, in Boston harbor, was named for his forebears. He would start conversations cold with "Speaking of David Thompson ... " and from there nothing would deter him—you had to wait him out, like a hurricane.

It must have been a shock to have the house suddenly full of teenagers who were more interested in Led Zeppellin than in David Thompson. I expect Grandpa was relieved when he moved to his quiet apartment in Capital Manor, the retirement home in Salem, where he could enjoy his genealogical records and his silence whenever he wanted it.

I didn't understand him then—I used to be one who needed the radio on all the time—but I think I do now. Except I think Grandpa, a man usually precise with his words, was a little bit wrong about what it was he craved: not silence, but stillness. There's a difference. When I travel in the car with John, we chat and then settle into a peaceful amity, not speaking and not needing to, just daydreaming to the music of the engine and the swishing of tires through the rain-filled ruts in the asphalt. That's stillness: full of little noises.

Sometimes, though, there is truly silence. One of us is moody or preoccupied. Or we are angry, one of us or both, and we deliberately break the current of affection between us, each turning it away from the other and inward, to energize our resentments and hurts. What is between us then is silence: vast, deep, empty.

I have talked to people who regularly meditate, and they tell me the goal of meditation is to experience the silence at the core of their being. They describe it as a complete unawareness of self coupled with a hyperawareness to things around them, perceiving these (but who or what does the perceiving? I wonder) as a mere kaleidoscope of phenomena, wisps of sound, dappled patterns of light, a moth bumbling around a light bulb, a single hair resting on the sleeve of a sweater, all occurring at once, outside of time, devoid of cause, effect, or meaning.

I've practiced meditation, trying to understand what this radical submersion of the self might feel like. My experience doesn't feel quite like silence to me. Self, in my case, is a kind of noise, or chattering. What I encounter when the chattering subsides is a deep and peaceful stillness. My mental self is quiet, but my bodily self is still present. My blood splashes through my vessels, and my breath sighs through my nostrils. I feel skin against damp skin, limb against bent limb; my tongue slides smooth over the inner surfaces of my teeth. When my thigh gets a cramp, when my stomach rumbles, I know it's my thigh, my stomach. I am still me: middle-aged, married, a daughter and a wife and a mother, a good cook, a middling gardener, and bearer of a host of other temporal meanings and limitations.

If there is silence at the core of my being, I am not sure I want to find it, for fear I will lose myself in it. Maybe that is what the great mystics are talking about. Silence, to me, sounds grand and alien, the environment of terrifying revelation, and I'm not sure I have the courage to confront it. "A vast silence reigned over the land," said Jack London. "The land itself was a desolation, lifeless, without movement, so lone and cold that the spirit of it was not even that of sadness ... It was the masterful and incommunicable wisdom of eternity laughing at the futility of life ..." He was speaking of the sublimely indifferent landscapes of Alaska, but his words apply as well to any monumental place, any place too hard for the tender human soul to endure.

The early Christian mystics sought to shed their soft selves in the silence of an austere landscape, not to escape reality but to find it. Yet is it necessary to lose oneself to find reality? I wonder. Because in the stillness at the core of my being I find myself. Or more precisely I find an acceptance of myself as good and necessary, an intrinsic part of the natural order. In this stillness, I am neither puffed up with my own importance nor flattened into an abject egolessness. I am just the right size, and I am in just the right place. Is this not reality?

Silence is wild, brutal, inhuman, sublime. It shocks us out of our bodily noisiness, pins our flapping limbs; it stuns us. It is Godly, terrifying. "The Lord is in His holy temple," intoned Habakkuk. "Let all the earth keep silence before Him." "We sleep to time's hurdy-gurdy," said Annie Dillard, "we wake, if we ever wake, to the silence of God."

Stillness is domestic. It is human, humble, soothing. "He leads me beside still waters; he restores my soul," said the Psalmist. "Peace, be still," said Jesus to the storm.

Silence is absence, emptiness, void. "The vast silence of interstellar space frightens me to death," said Antoine de St.-Exupéry. Stillness is presence, quiet sights and sounds, the touch of a hand, the music of voices, a canoe gliding over quiet waves, parting the water not with the terrible stroke of a rod but with a quiet bow-thrust and a rhythmic splash of paddle.

I believe it wasn't silence Grandpa craved, but stillness. Now, sixteen years after he died, I'm still here in his house, and I love the stillnesses I imagine he loved: the songs of coyotes and frogs, the scratching of quail under the blueberries, and the hollow scrape of wind through the panes of the greenhouse. I think of him whenever I snap off the radio so I can listen to the rain coming down.

Tryouts

Early in the spring I took my daughter to softball tryouts. We gathered at the weedy field just east of the elementary school, seventy or eighty girls and a handful of coaches, parents, grandparents, big and little siblings, and dogs, assembled to watch.

"Mary Wells?" said the Little League coordinator, all business. She has known my daughter since Mary was a toddler, but she consulted her clipboard. "I don't have you here. I can't give you a number unless you're here."

"I was late getting the check in," I said.

"Okay." She scribbled on the clipboard. "Turn around." She pinned a paper number onto Mary's back. "Just tell Coach your registration's coming, and he'll take care of you."

The girls were herded into a ragged line by four men wearing baseball caps that said "MIKI," which stands for Monmouth-Independence Kids, Inc.

"Okay, girls, listen up," said one of them. "We're going to be watching how you play, and we're also going to be watching how you act, what kind of team player you are. So be on your best behavior."

The first year Mary played, spring was late and the parents shivered through four wet weeks of practices and games, our jeans soaking up the rainwater from the spongy bleachers. The weather encouraged a sort of foxhole camaraderie among us; it was a season of shared blankets, umbrellas, and thermoses of coffee. But this was a good day for tryouts, moist and misty, dry enough that the winter puddles around the bases had shrunk down to sheeny slicks, warm enough for the girls to be wearing shorts. The sun pushing through the thin clouds made the bleachers steam a little.

The field was full of half-grown girls horsing around with paper numbers pinned to their backs. There is a lot of variety in size and shape among girls of eleven and twelve, which is all the more noticeable because of the pains they take to conceal it: the carefully casual, curly-banged ponytails, the floppy shorts and loose-tailed t-shirts, the high-priced athletic sneakers with two sets of laces each. Underneath this protective coloration is a girl who probably looks less like her contemporaries at this age than at any other. This is the time of life when a girl's differences are most vulnerable to the brutal judgments of her peers.

Here at softball tryouts the judgments are simple and universally affirmed: Can you hit? Can you throw? Can you catch? Softball is a meritocracy—everybody knows good playing when they see it, and if you don't have what it takes, the pain is clean and quick, not like the slow agony, a couple of years later, of the girl who fails to make another sort of team, who can't seem to get the hang of the tacit and impenetrable rules of the game.

The girls field fly balls, shag grounders, throw from first to third, bat balls from the tops of metal tees. Then they line up to swing at balls pitched by the coaches. The coaches look them over, making notes. "Treat this just like a game, girls," calls the head coach. "We want to see you give it a hundred and ten percent."

We parents talk in a desultory way, not saying much of importance but sharing freely, like strangers on an airplane, and our conversation has the same fleeting intimacy to it. There is a democracy among us, too, that comes of being peripheral to the main action; our children are the stars. Another girl's mother tells me a long story about her daughter's troubles in school. I don't know this woman, and I know her daughter only as one of the medium-sized figures out there on the field, but I nod and mm-hmm in empathy. Whose child has not had troubles in school?

The conversation puts me in mind of that first cold season and a conversation with another mother who I'd hoped would become my friend. Sharing a damp blanket on the bleachers, we talked about her profession (psychiatric nursing) and mine (journalism, then), our goals for ourselves, our hopes for our children. I told her, "This is a hard town to make friends in," astonished that I dared to say it, hoping that this time I might have better luck. I didn't, though. Once her husband borrowed my husband's socket-wrench set; another time I invited them to dinner and she declined. These and the bleacher conversations have been the extent of our relationship in the larger social world of this town, where the rules of engagement are ambiguous and subject to misinterpretation.

But I'm glad to see her at a ballgame. We always have a nice chat, and I've learned that a circumscribed relationship is better than none. A base hit may not be a home run, but it beats striking out.

Sports is the social context for most adult gatherings in my town. We have our children in common, if not much else perhaps. We yell encouragement from the bleachers, and we go for pizza to celebrate a victory. We gather at post-season parties to drink beers and sodas on the patio, remembering the season's high moments, weaving long reveries—sagas, almost—about the time one of the dads needled the umpire so brutally that the umpire finally yanked off his cap, threw it down on home plate, and stomped off the field; about the time the team's best pitcher broke a tie, and her ankle, sliding into home in the bottom of the ninth. These gatherings don't demand any subtle social skills.

There seems to be a notion among city people that life in a small town is friendly and cozy. That's what I expected to find, anyway, when we moved here from Seattle. Maybe this is true in the first stage, the getting-to-know-you stage. We are great at hailing each other in grocery store parking lots, standing and gabbing in the checkout line. But when this superficiality begins to weary me, when it's time to move on to the work of making a relationship, I have found it tough going. Maybe the very commonness of everyday encounters makes us wary—if we commit too soon, we may have to renege later, and in a small town you can't hide from your social miscalculations. Or—maybe it's just me. Or maybe I just can't get the hang of the rules here. Maybe I'm not giving it a hundred and ten percent.

I settled back to watch the last event of the tryouts. Mary stepped up to the plate, poised and tense, choking up a little on the bat. The pitcher sent the ball in fast and a little high, a straight-on meatball, and Mary hit it clean and solid, a line drive into right center field. She trotted to first base, looking bored. I remembered my own sixth-grade softball humiliations—the feeble infield grounders, the muffed flies, the exile to far left field. My clean-limbed and graceful daughter looked like she knew what she was doing out there, and I was happy for her. If you can play ball in this town, you're home free.

Memorial Day

On the Friday before Memorial Day Gavin walked into the kitchen and announced, "I have a chicken in my room."

"A chicken?" I said.

"I brought it home from biology class. It just hatched this morning. We're supposed to watch how they grow over the weekend and write a report. I'll show you."

He went downstairs to his room, clumping in his size-eleven sneakers hard enough to make noise on the concrete steps. Gavin turned sixteen last February, and he's getting to the place where his body are evening out—arms and legs roughly proportional, height and feet at about the right ratio.

He came back up with a shoebox with holes in the lid. He set the box down on the dining-room table and took the top off, slowly. Inside the box, huddled on torn newspaper, was the day-old chick. It was covered with silky down the color of beaten egg yolks. It had a long neck and protruding eyes still masked with membrane and a beak and feet so big that, like Tweety Pie's, they seemed comically large for its frail body. Gavin scooped it up and cuddled it in his palms.

"Are you supposed to pick them up?" I asked nervously.

"Oh, sure," he said. "See, he's cold." The chick was shivering, and I remembered that baby chicks needed to be kept warm if their mothers couldn't rear them. Gradually the chick settled down in Gavin's hands. It stopped shivering and seemed to go to sleep. Then it started awake, jerked its head up, and peeped feebly.

We got a heating pad and a lamp and a thermometer left over from the time we raised lambs out in the tractor shed. Gavin didn't know how warm the chick needed to be, so we consulted one of our farming manuals. It told us to keep the box at ninety-five degrees. We checked on the chick every few minutes, adjusting the lamp, turning the heating pad up or down. Gavin sprinkled down some grit and seed he had brought with him from school, and he filled the cap of a milk jug with water, which the chick kept knocking over.

The chick was funny to watch. It would stand up, tottering on its big scaly feet and flapping its nubbins of wings, and issue two or three weak bleats. Then it would nod off to sleep like an old man after dinner. A few seconds later it would jerk itself awake and begin the whole process again.

The chick's presence disrupted the dailiness of our lives. It ushered into our house a sense of extraordinary urgency; all normal routine was suspended in favor of nurturing this chick. The chick carried in its tiny body the ferocious imperative of life—life not to be trifled with, life not to be taken lightly. It was a responsibility imposed by fate, and we were as obligated as if we'd encountered an accident on the highway. I am in this time; I am in this place; I must save this life.

On Saturday I planted my warm-season vegetables—corn and beans and squash, tomatoes and peppers and cantaloupes. Some people get theirs in earlier, but the climate in this part of the world is too unreliable to count on warm soil much before June. The ground was still too wet to till properly, but we tilled anyway, and so we wound up with that peculiar lumpy Willamette Valley mud, the kind that, when it dries, makes clods you can flatten only with the back of a shovel.

It was cold and the garden didn't seem ready for tomatoes. I scrabbled a little compost into each hole before laying the plant carefully in—bending the lower stem to bury it sideways, horizontally, so roots would form all along it. I was worried that the cloddy soil would shock the tender plants. But they were getting leggy and needed to go into the ground.

Every now and then I'd look in on the chick. It seemed to be gaining strength, staying awake for longer stretches, pecking at seeds with its big beak, flapping its ridiculous little wings, sometimes drowsing with its head bumping the edge of its water dish. I cooed softly to it and stroked its throat with my finger, trying to get it to peep.

It took me until dinnertime to finish planting. A cold wind had come up out of the west, pushing steel-colored clouds before it. I knew I wouldn't have to water the new plants. I surveyed the tomatoes, upright but limp in their steel cages, their leaves palely reflecting the twilight, and hoped they'd make it.

On Sunday morning it was obvious that the chick had declined during the night. It didn't look good. It would slip from a crouch, its usual drowsing position, to lying flat on its side, its head cocked back at an angle. The chick looked pulled-down, poured-out, as if gravity were winning the tug-of-war with life in its slip of a body. Occasionally it would raise its head and try to peep, but the efforts grew feebler and feebler.

Inside me the anxiety was building. It felt like one of those nightmares where something terrible is chasing you and you can't run. I wanted desperately to turn things around. Let's force it to drink some water. Let's give it more food. Let's turn up the heating pad. Let's do something, for God's sake! But finally I just watched, helpless, as life flowed out of the chick's slack body.

On Monday I got up early to gather flowers for the family graves. When I was younger, Memorial Day for me was nothing more than a three-day weekend, a time to relax from school or work. Lately, though, I've grown more thoughtful about these things. Maybe I'm hungrier now for connectedness with the people whose genes, quirks, passions, and dreams live on in me. Maybe it's because, having lived about half my expected life span, I'm becoming more aware that I will one day join them. I was looking forward to tidying the graves and setting flowers next to the stones and saying a little prayer—although for whom, I wasn't sure.

I took three plastic gallon-sized milk jugs and cut off the tops around the front and sides, leaving the handles for carrying. I found my pruners and cut purple and yellow irises, sweet Williams, wild daisies, and some ferns for greens. The irises were planted by my grandmother years ago when my garden belonged to her. I arranged the flowers—not very expertly—in the milk jugs, filled the jugs with water, and wedged them in with some empty boxes on the floor of the car.

The Fircrest cemetery is just a couple of miles from our house. There are three family graves there. I felt that Grandma, if she could see me at her gravesite, would be pleased with the flowers, especially since she had planted some of them, and, because she was a frugal and practical woman, she wouldn't mind the milk jugs. Grandpa wouldn't care about either the flowers or the milk jugs, but he would be pleased to see me.

As for my father—well, it was hard to tell with him. He was a man of changing moods, sometimes a brooding anger that came out cutting and sarcastic, just as often a mute despair. And sometimes he was warm and loving and funny. Sometimes he'd know exactly how you felt, and he'd give you exactly what you needed. He'd be glad to see me, I told myself, and he'd probably like the flowers, too.

I remembered visiting him in the VA hospital in the last weeks of his life. I remembered the waxy slackness of his cheeks and the way gravity seemed to be sucking him down into his hospital bed. After he died my sister said he'd told her he wanted to be buried at the cemetery near our house instead of in Coos Bay with the rest of his family, his mother and his infant brother. He did not tell me this. My sister Leslie said he told her, but I have always wondered how he told her, because they had taken out his cancerous larynx and he couldn't talk. I have always wondered if my sister made this up, just to make me feel better. It did make me feel better.

We buried him up at the cemetery on an April morning. I stood dry-eyed by the grave. We had an Episcopal burial service, although Dad had never been religious. "In my father's house are many mansions," read the priest from the gospel of John. "I go to prepare a place for you."

My grandparents' gravestones are marked with nothing more than their names and their birth and death years. My father's has these things and also, because the Veterans' Administration bought his gravestone, the inscription "Ensign U.S.N." Other graves, especially the older ones and those of children, are more generously inscribed: "Called to be with God." "In the arms of Jesus." "We'll meet in Heaven." Death is the commonest thing in the world, but it's hard to see it that way when it touches you. When I look at a tiny chick ebbing life I feel outrage, then bitter defeat. Chicks die every day, yet I feel this little death touching all the big deaths in my memory. It's a feeling so strong that I imagine it even calls up the genetic memory of all my dead ancestors, living on somewhere in my tissues, my cells.

As I came home from the cemetery, I saw Gavin headed for the back garden in his dad's size-extra-large oilskin jacket, a shovel in one hand, a shoebox in the other. It was a cool, misty morning, and the day promised more rain. Gavin started to dig. I watched him make a hole about a foot deep. Then he reached into the box, picked up the chick's body, and laid it softly in the hole. The tomato plants still looked pale, but I thought they were standing up a little straighter.

Frugal

My mother was raised in the Great Depression, and the frugality she learned in childhood has stayed with her. She reuses her teabags. She won't chew a whole stick of gum. When she bakes cookies, she says, "Now, what else could we put in the oven with these?" I remember this from when I was a child learning to cook. Whenever we baked cookies, we'd also have to get a pot roast or a chicken ready for the oven, or mix up some cornbread. Mom had learned to cook on a wood stove. If I suggested just baking the cookies, just the cookies, she would look at me with shocked disapproval: "You can't light an oven for just one thing." This tendency sometimes led her down a path of rationalization. She'd stick in a pan of biscuits alongside a tuna casserole, even if biscuits weren't on the menu. "We can eat them for breakfast," she'd say. From her I learned to want what I could get. Conversely, I learned not to want what wasn't worth turning on the oven for, all by itself.

I'm not a gum-chewer, but I do reuse teabags. I save zipper-top plastic sacks and yogurt containers and jam jars that have the little sealing dimple in the lid. You can preserve several batches of jam in these before the rubber lid lining crumbles. I reuse paper bags until they're too fragile to hold any weight. I trim the elastic bands from worn-out pairs of underpants; the fabric makes good cleaning rags and the elastic bands hold appliance cords in a neat sheaf. I save my egg cartons for the neighbor who raises chickens. Sometimes I hear myself going on like this, and I think, *What am I, poor?* I get impatient with myself; I feel vaguely ashamed. Because sometimes I do carry it too far. I wear sweaters with holes in them. I put up with broken light fixtures and chipped coffee cups. I make do.

John's family was better fixed than mine. When we were first married, I was amazed at his mother's attitude toward worldly possessions. She was extravagant, I thought. When an appliance broke, she went right out and got it fixed, or bought a new one. She didn't work around the problem; she didn't make do; she didn't substitute some lesser fix. It never occurred to her that she didn't need a working dishwasher, or that she ought to do without. She just called the repairman, and that was that.

When John and I were married, we had a very small wedding budget. I didn't know the merchants in Seattle as well as my mother-in-law did, so I asked her to choose the florist and the bakery for the cake. I would have been fine going to Safeway for both, but Vernice chose a boutique bakery on Queen Anne Hill that specialized in wedding cakes, and an exclusive flower shop in Ballard. She liked things that were "nice"—not inexpensive.

My mother, on the other hand, taught me how to unit-price canned tomatoes, and today I reflexively choose the store brand of almost anything. Grandpa fixed up this house from lumber and windows scavenged from the ruined parts of it that he tore down. He built his walls sturdy, but the wall studs, just for one example, aren't always right where they should be. Sometimes Grandpa didn't have pieces of the size he needed, so he scabbed together the studs from too-short pieces of two-by-four. He made do. His frugality afforded only the necessities—anything superfluous in his house was a luxury.

He left our basement walls unfinished, with light-switch boxes popping out at the ends of conduits that snaked down from the ceiling, secured to the plaster walls with big staples. Lights were bare bulbs with pull strings. The basement bathroom was three feet wide and six feet long. It was dim and smelly, and the upstairs plumbing hung down below the floor joists. The toilet sat on a wooden platform six inches above the floor, so there'd be enough fall in the line to convey the wastewater downhill to the septic tank. The floor boards were spongy from years of leaks and overflows. Grandpa's water came from a well, and there was not quite enough when our large family gathered at Elkins Road for Thanksgiving. He told us, "Don't flush the toilet until it's absolutely necessary." You could look up from that toilet and see networks of cobwebs amid the grimy pipes, and the rough tongue-and-groove boards of the underside of the upstairs floor with dust sifting down through.

When we were kids, we were forcefully encouraged to use the basement bathroom. The grownups didn't want us tracking mud through the upstairs. We could just come in the basement door and use the bathroom down there—what was so hard about that? *It smells, and there are spiders,* we could have said, but we just ducked in there when we seriously had to go, and we did our business quickly.

When my three younger sisters were living here with my mother, the downstairs bathroom was theirs. By this time it had been painted Harvest Gold, with paint left over from the outside of the house. Laurie, the artist in our family, had received for Christmas a book of Great Paintings of the European Masters. The book came with a sheaf of colored pictures printed on thick paper. Laurie stapled the pictures to the bathroom wall, edge to edge, hiding the orange paint as best she could. You could sit down there as long as you wanted, breathing through your mouth, and study Titian's red-haired girls and Rubens' rosy nudes. Those pictures were still there when John and I moved in. I took them down a few years later. I couldn't bear to throw them away, so I stuck them in an envelope and put them away somewhere. I painted the walls white, but that did not improve things much. The toilet still stank, and it still rocked on its foundation.

We'd been thinking about fixing up that bathroom for a long time. We got a head of steam going a couple of years ago and turned off the water and took the toilet out and left it sitting in the middle of the basement floor. We removed the spindle-legged old sink and, amazingly, took it to the dump. We wanted to take out the toilet platform, too, and make the bathroom floor flat, level with the rest of the basement. But that would have involved jackhammering out the concrete and then digging the drain line again, putting it deeper into the ground. And then we would have to plumb the new bathroom completely from scratch, a complicated job that John didn't feel up to.

A couple of plumbers were called. One of them, after hearing the situation, said vaguely that he'd think about it and call us back. He never did. The other plumber came out, glanced at the bathroom, mentioned a large sum of money, said he'd get back to us, and never did.

We left that bathroom sitting, gutted, for way too long. We were scared to tackle it. We wanted too much. We wanted a flat floor. We wanted a shower—how could we shoehorn a shower into that tiny space? We wanted to move the washer and dryer out of the main part of the basement and replumb them into John's workshop on the other side of the bathroom wall.

There was just too much to think about, and one thing we really didn't want to think about was how much money it would cost. So we avoided the issue. We pretended it wasn't so important. We got used to stepping around the toilet in the middle of the basement, and finally moved it closer to the sewing machine to get it out of the way. There it sat for two years, like a shipwreck.

One day a cat got into the basement. John saw it come in, and he recognized it as the feral cat that regularly beats up on our cat and makes her squeal during the night. The cat sneaked in through the basement door, eluded our chase, and finally leaped up on top of the water heater and then up into the joists. It picked its way across the top of the basement's unfinished walls and disappeared down inside the bathroom wall. We could hear it scrabbling for purchase. "That's enough," John said. He took a crowbar and a sledge hammer and began ripping the walls off the studs. I opened the back door. When John's crowbar came to where the cat was, it blinked and streaked out. It took a wild cat to make us do what we'd been avoiding for so long.

As he tore out the inner walls, John made a disconcerting discovery: a pile of mouse skeletons at the bottom of the wall. What had happened, Grandpa had left a gap in the horizontal stringer. For years the mice had run along the two-by-four inside the wall, fallen off the cliff at the end, and landed on the pile. It was an awful thing to contemplate, all those mice dying slow deaths in the dark, at the bottom of a pit, on top of skeletons of other mice. But no doubt that was where some of the smell had been coming from.

With the bathroom's walls and plumbing piled out in the backyard, we were committed. John dismantled the west partition and rebuilt it two feet out, making room for a small shower. The new partition met the foundation wall at right angles, right in the middle of a window, so he took out the glass and built a vertical mullion in the center and put in two oblongs of frosted glass. He moved the washer and dryer around to the shop side and plumbed them in across from his table saw. Next to the washer he put in a deep sink. "We have a mud room!" I exulted. "Okay, but it's still my shop, too," John said. We get a little sawdust in the dryer filter, and that's okay with me.

In the enlarged bathroom space he built a stair-stepped platform. You step up one diagonal step, past a discreet wing wall, and there's the toilet; another zig-step and there's the shower. It's elegant. The shower has a window to let the sun in and a wall of glass brick on the other side, and it's lined with pale-peach ceramic tile. The walls and trim are painted in shades of ginger—I can hardly help breaking into a decorator-magazine gush—and the floor is a swirl of blue and peach linoleum. What's more, it's smooth: John patched the rough concrete before he laid it down.

We got the linoleum on sale. I bought the shower tile at a garage sale a long time ago, knowing it would come in handy some day. We used the sink and cabinet that were once in Grandpa's bedroom upstairs. We put the old toilet back in. I sat there on the basement floor in rubber gloves and scrubbed it with a brush, until all the crusty ancient soil and mold was gone and nothing remained but a faint calcium ring.

We had to buy some of the materials new. The glass brick alone made me catch my breath: seven dollars apiece for the square, rough-edged bricks, and thirteen for the bullnosed ones. We could have scrabbled together enough recycled boards to use for the baseboard trim, but what the heck! John bought new ones. And then there was the window glass, and the drywall, and the mortar and grout for the tile. It added up.

There is a frugality that puts up with smelly bathrooms and broken light switches and doorless cabinets and cracked linoleum and mismatched plates. There is a frugality that pushes desires out of the mind, denies wanting anything for fear of the cost. That kind of frugality doesn't bake a cake unless there's a pot roast to put in alongside it.

"If wishes were horses, then beggars would ride," said my mother. "It isn't what you want that makes you fat, it's what you get," said my Auntie Pat. There's a frugality that says it's better not to want at all, lest you be found unworthy of having and your heart be broken. That kind of frugality says, Blessed are they that expect nothing, for they will never be disappointed. That kind of frugality can't afford innocent delight or sensuous desire.

Then there is a frugality that celebrates beauty and utility and doesn't accept makeshift or almost-good-enough. I don't mean luxury; I don't mean conspicuous consumption. I mean elegance—a frugality that gives you enough, with grace and generosity. That is the frugality of being modest in your wants. Our new bathroom is frugal, but it is also beautiful, and things work.

Race Pace

The other morning I woke up, as I often do on a Saturday, mentally writing a to-do list: scrub bathroom, write essay, wash dog, make applesauce, can tomatoes, cart out recycling. Usually I make a mental time-and-motion study out of it—arrange the tasks in the most efficient order, and then, at the end of the day, savor the strung-out high that comes from ticking them all off the list.

Instead, though, I rode the seventy miles to the ocean with John to watch Gavin run in a cross-country race on the beach. It was a hasty decision, and I felt some regret after it was too late to turn back. On the way over I hoped the race wouldn't last too long. Maybe I could salvage some of my plans for the afternoon; maybe get some writing done, at least.

The race was on a stretch of beach that angles out into the surf. It is a wide, shallow apron of sand, so that when the tide is low, as it was that morning, the sea is a long way out and wide pools of seawater stretch between the surf and the dry sand. The pools glimmered gauzily in the hazy sunshine.

The runners moved in restless clumps near the starting line, forming and reforming like schools of fish. Now and then one of them would sprint off, loop around, and rejoin the clump. As I strolled up the beach, looking for shells, a couple of racers burst past me, startling me a little. Five rangy boys walked onto the wet sand, their bright yellow singlets and shorts making long, sun-colored streaks on the water sheen behind them.

The race was a three-thousand-meter run up the beach and back. Gavin overestimated his race pace and started out too fast, and he got a stitch in the side that slowed him down on the home stretch. He came in thirty-fourth out of thirty-nine runners.

Gavin was well into his teens, past the age when a mother's hug helps much. Still, I was glad I had come. I hope that, when he gets to be forty and starts feeling sentimental about his childhood, he'll remember I was there after that disappointing run.

Starting when our children were very young, John and I used to take them to museums and concerts to broaden them, expose them to experiences they wouldn't necessarily seek out on their own. I didn't realize until much later that it is they who are broadening us. These children take me places that, left to myself, I would never go—Stockton, California, for one. Last summer Mary played softball in a tournament in that sprawling, untidy agricultural town, not the sort of place you'd choose to spend a mid-August weekend. We parents sweated and cheered and sipped tepid water in unshaded bleachers and watched our daughters lose three games in a row. I took two vacation days for that trip, two days I hadn't planned on and really couldn't spare away from work, not right then. I had reports to edit, brochures to lay out, places to go, people to see. Instead, I slowed the pace of my life down to the lazy arc of a pop fly, got sunburned lips, and learned to scream, "Slide, slide, slide!" without inhibition.

Race pace is the speed that gives a runner a shot at winning without collapsing on the way. At race pace, you feel primed with energy; your joints feel loose and your movements easy. Your muscles are alert but not tense, your attention is focused on the next step in front of you, and your solar plexus hums like a tuned engine.

Race pace is a calculated balance of speed and endurance. Go too slow and you're jogging—good enough for practice and when you want to take it easy, but it won't win you a race. Go too fast—"barf pace," Gavin calls it—and your calf will cramp, or your side will ache, or your wind will fail, and you'll lose.

Most days I calculate my own race pace pretty well. I unfold my mental time-and-motion chart as I open my office door: These three phone calls should take twenty minutes, and then I can spend two hours on the gene-research story, and by that time the annual report layout should have arrived, and if I proof the first ten pages before noon I can fax them over to Newport before the secretary leaves for lunch, and then I can pick up the brochure proof from the printers' and swing by the drugstore and pick up John's prescription and only be a little late for the one o'clock meeting, but I'll have to remember to avoid the road construction on Kings Boulevard ... And when I get home the blueberries need pruning ...

And I move from one task to the next, focused, primed, my engine humming, and I get to the end of the day and feel that spacy satisfaction of having survived a marathon, the rush that comes from imposing my will on my circumstances and watching them submit.

And then some days the phone calls take forty minutes instead of twenty, and there are twenty pages to proof instead of ten, and the fax machine is down, and the meeting is moved up, and so I run harder and I get a stitch in my side and my wind fails and I get stuck behind a truck on Kings Boulevard, and I lose the race, I lose bad, and nobody's hug makes any difference.

What I forget is that I don't have to race all the time. What reminds me of this is the grace of necessary interruptions, those trips I would not choose to take, left to myself. Though I do not accept it gracefully, grace comes to me through cross-country races at the beach and softball games in Stockton and the need to go to the sporting goods store *right this minute* to buy a gym bag.

Gavin gets up every school morning at six o'clock so he can get to jazz band practice at seven. Cross-country practice is every day after school until five o'clock, and there's at least one meet every week, sometimes two; but when there isn't a meet he has pep band practice Tuesdays and Thursdays from five till six, and then he plays with the pep band at the football games on Friday nights. John and I look at each other ironically, and say, *Where does he get that?* but I know where he gets it.

He doesn't know this, but he is teaching me a lesson he hasn't learned yet. I wonder if his eldest child will some day teach him the same lesson—that there are days when you don't have to race, days when the race is of no importance next to the sight of five high-school boys playing in the surf, making long golden streaks along the shore.

Halloween

Dinnertime came as I was driving home from Tillamook on Halloween night, so I stopped in a small town for pizza. It was chilly and dark, and the air smelled like frost and wood smoke. The sidewalks of the town swarmed with little kids dressed as ballerinas and pirates and Ninja Turtles, and big kids whose only costume was a perfunctory mask or makeup job and a large plastic bag. The little kids were accompanied by their parents, who were costumed, too, something I didn't do when my children were little. I saw a short woman with bright red circles on her cheeks and a blond wig and enormous balloon breasts. She was dragging two little kids by the hand. "Hurry up," she snapped at them, jerking their arms as they negotiated the curb, a completely-in-character exasperated mother absurdly painted to resemble a streetwalker. In the pizza parlor a tall man with a Groucho Marx mustache and false nose studied the menu. A clown crossed the floor with two floppy paper plates of pizza and set one of the plates down before a small lion with a tail that swept the floor.

I read a story in the business pages recently that Halloween is not just a kids' celebration any more, it's a marketing bonanza. More adults are now costuming themselves for parties, even for work. On Halloween day, John sat in a meeting with Cleopatra. It was hard, he told me, to talk about software bugs with anybody wearing a snake headpiece.

I understand the appeal, though. This year John and I spent twenty dollars apiece for two cheesy pieces of foam-backed polyester printed to look like playing cards, the King and Queen of Hearts. We sprayed our hair red and painted our faces like mimes and went to a dance. People laughed and said ours were the best costumes there. "You look beautiful," whispered one man as we danced, "with that jazzy red lipstick." He said this not to my real, middle-aged, usually sensible self, but to the character I had turned myself into, a fantasy queen, powerful, remote, ageless.

Halloween costumes are supposed to be the modern expression of an ancient impulse to frighten away evil spirits at the darkening time of the year. Later the Christian church tried to tame that dread into a sober recognition of the faithful departed. Catholics and Episcopalians celebrate the communion of saints on the first of November, All Saints' Day. But the pagan impulse is not so easily subsumed. We buy plastic facsimiles of the faces of Porky Pig and Bart Simpson, and we put them on at the office and at pizza parlors and parties, on the street with our kids on Halloween night, laughing at our own absurdity, clinging for one night to a different persona, one that is beyond the realm of everyday life, which is to say, one that cannot be touched by death.

Some people wear costumes for the opposite reason, to remind us of impending death, or at least that's what they say. These are the young people you see in the coffee bars and the underage dance clubs wearing all-black clothes, black-dyed hair, dead-white faces, and, in the case of the girls, blood-red lipstick. I heard some of them explaining it on a radio talk show. "We Goths see ourselves as the cultural inheritors of the fin-de-siècle tradition of the late nineteenth century," said a seventeen-year-old girl in a whispery voice, earnest as an anthropologist. "We're a subculture of a society that spends a lot of energy denying death. When we dress up in black and wear white makeup and read decadent Romantic poetry, it's to confront society with the reality that death is always with us."

The Goths don't regard this as morbid, added a young man, but theatrical, a big send-up. "We're mocking the achiever-oriented values of this culture. Our presence reminds people to live each day to the fullest." The breathy young woman added, "I'm really a very happy person."

Listening, I reflected on the delicious luxury of being young and remote enough from death to be able to treat it as a virtue, like exercising or vegetarianism; to be able to lecture one's elders about their frivolous avoidance of it, *you really should face this; it's for your own good.* Older, I now know that honesty is not the only tactic, nor necessarily always the best one. A little creative denial lifts the spirits, especially when it allows you to prance around in red tights and a horned skullcap and a sly little tail.

∽∽

A few weeks before Halloween I dug up a rhododendron in our side yard. It had been in the way for a long time, and I wanted to move it around to the front. I started with a spade and began chipping ineffectually at the clayey bed. Then I switched to a mattock, a tool with a flat sharp blade on one side and a pick on the other. I chopped a trench around the drip line, lifting the mattock high above my head and bringing it down with all my force, pausing after each six or eight strokes to breathe hard. Then I wiggled a shovel down into the narrow opening and scooped dirt out onto a ten-by-twenty-foot plastic tarpaulin. Then back to the mattock: *whack whack whack whack whack*, then lean and pant and stretch the back muscles, then *whack whack whack* some more. It was the hardest work I've ever done. After two hours of it, my back was screaming.

Finally I was able to wiggle the rhododendron loose. I hoisted it up out of its hole onto another tarp, dragged it to its new hole, and carefully tamped it in, saying a little prayer: *Please survive the winter.* And then I sat on the ground and rested, conscious of the mortal ache in my knees and elbows and lower back; not in the muscles, where a younger person might expect to feel the exertion, but in the joints, those places where the body unknits itself in preparation for the long night.

After a few minutes I rose creakily and went back into the side yard to contemplate the mound on the tarp, and the gaping hole. The dirt looked fluffed and shaken, plumped, like a feather comforter. Surely there was more dirt on that tarp than had ever been in the hole. Yet as I shoveled the dirt back in, it settled down obligingly, tamping itself, leaving only the slightest mound, a neat oval, like the top of a new loaf of bread.

Water

The winter rains have been unrelenting this year, as usual; not savage and stormy, just constant water dripping out of constant dull skies, wearing you down with irritation and ennui, like a leaky faucet. This is the legendary raininess of western Oregon, the kind that grays the faces of old-timers and makes newcomers ask fretfully, *Does it ever stop raining here?* The river spills over into the clayey, low-lying farm fields near our house and sits there like water in a stopped-up sink. Driving to work last week, I saw a lake where a field used to be, water melting down the plowed ridges of earth and chewing on islands of hay bales stacked ten high. The Luckiamute, the color of café mocha, lapped turgidly at the bridge pilings, carrying tree limbs and clots of brush ripped from bankside bushes, sucking and swirling them lazily toward the Willamette. The constant gray drizzle gets to you, I don't care how long you've lived here. Small annoyances enrage; petty blues ratchet quickly to despair.

Our bathtub drain has been plugged since Valentine's Day. This house has some idiosyncratic features, including a drain line with three ninety-degree corners and no fall for the first ten feet or so. Two applications of lye and several snakings didn't dislodge the clog. John even dismantled one of the pipe corners and sprayed a hose down the line at full force. No improvement.

Our showers got shorter and shorter—none of us relished standing ankle-deep in tepid, scummy water. This is a minor annoyance except during the gray season; then it produces sulking and swearing and slamming of doors. I've lived through quite a few Februaries in the Willamette Valley, and I try to stay on my best behavior, but I was ready to use dynamite on that damned drain.

On the twenty-fifth, a Friday, we celebrated Gavin's birthday. Every now and then on Thursday evening I dipped into my memory: Seventeen years ago *right now* I was fixing dinner, and then, Seventeen years ago *right now* I was getting ready for bed, not knowing that this would be the night. We lived on the Canadian prairie, and earth, river, and sky were frozen solid. Seventeen years ago *right now* I got up to go to the bathroom and felt the waters break and flow out of me. I stood there in the dim hallway, calling, John? John? Frightened: Is it ever going to stop? And then, immediately, faint but sure, I felt contractions and a sudden exhilarating anticipation. Now the waiting was over. Now things were moving.

We're all edgy this winter. John has been looking for work since the end of July. We are careful to keep our spirits up, for our own and the kids' sake, but sometimes our morale rises and falls like the creeks. The kids seem to be handling the situation well—maybe a little too well. Shouldn't they be acting out more?

"Hey, Mom," Mary said, looking up from her algebra homework. "Do you remember that time Gavin tried to drown me?"

What?

"Wait a minute," said Gavin. "I wasn't trying to drown you. I was just playing a joke."

"What?" I said.

On another waterlogged February day, when Gavin was six and Mary three, they were playing down near the woods. The creek had overflowed, and the first row of trees was standing in water. Gavin found a wooden fruit crate.

"Hey, Mary," he said. "Here's a boat. Want to take a boat ride?"

Obligingly, Mary stepped into the box. "Here you go!" said Gavin, shoving the box into the water. It sank immediately, of course, leaving Mary standing up to her hips in dirty water. She climbed out of the box and waded after Gavin, too angry to cry.

"Don't you remember?" Mary asked. I didn't remember, and I was horrified that I didn't. *How much have these children endured in this place?* I asked myself.

"I was probably too little to tell on him," said Mary. Seeing my face, she said, "Relax, Mom. I wasn't hurt, I was just mad."

John is waiting for word on a job in Portland, seventy miles away. He's had three interviews. I try to put it out of my mind, but the suspense is killing me. Portland! So far away. Endlessly we discuss it. We could move there—but there's my job, and the kids' school ... Well, we could move a little closer. Salem, maybe. That way I could keep my job and the kids could stay in school with their friends.

Move. (I don't know ...) Sell this house? (No! But ...) Well, then, rent the house? Maybe—but could we afford to rent anywhere else?

Could John carpool? Could he take the bus? Could he stay over in Portland a couple of nights a week? Could he work four ten-hour days? Could he ...? The talk meanders. And then John points out, "I don't even have the job yet. Let's cross that bridge when we come to it."

On Friday morning John goes after the bathtub clog again. This time he pushes the snake down through the tub's overflow drain. Listening outside the door, I hear a gurgle and a swoosh and the faucet running for a long time.

On Friday evening the phone rings. John takes it downstairs. After a long time he comes up and tells me he's beaten out the other two candidates for the job in Portland. "It's still not absolutely certain," he says. "I have to meet one more guy and they have to check my references. And I have to take a drug test, if you can believe that. But I'm the top pick, and it sounds good." His face has lost its February pallor, and there is a lightness in his blue eyes.

Driving to work on Monday, I see that the water in the flooded fields has receded, leaving wrinkled mud flats and soggy hay bales. Here and there in the higher grass, a pane of water glints silver-blue, reflecting the softer, lighter sky.

Slimy Dead Pumpkins

❧❦

On a drizzly Saturday the chatter inside my head was getting troublesome. *This place is a mess. Look at the dirt on those windows. You should have painted those windowsills before it started raining. The bathroom is a disgrace. I'm not even mentioning the vegetable garden. Slimy dead pumpkins and black ropy tomato vines and weeds, weeds. Yuck. Why didn't you clean it up last fall? What's wrong with you?* It was too wet to plow or plant, too warm to stay inside, so I wandered out to look for something to do.

I started by dumping out the wheelbarrow, flushing a flood of rainwater and a black mass of mouldering cherry leaves out on top of the rotten pumpkins. Then I wheeled down to the orchard and started picking up sticks from the winter's pruning—grape, apple, pear—and laying them on the burn pile. *You never finished the pruning. Why do you always put things off? You know it makes you feel like crap.*

Yes, I agreed with myself. It does.

Finding myself near the woodshed, I sorted through the firewood, picking out pieces too big for the woodstove and laying them in a rough pile. I decided to fill the woodbox while I was at it, and as I wheelbarrowed across the lawn I noticed the pile of maple leaves lying where they'd been dumped last fall. *You should have picked them up right away. They'll leave a bare spot.*

Lay off, I told myself irritably. The grass will come back.

I filled the wheelbarrow with leaves and considered where to put them. Maple leaves are tough and leathery, and they decompose slowly. If they'll kill grass, I thought, let's put them where we want to kill the grass. My eye fell on the strip of tough, half-wild climbing roses that Grandma had planted next to the road. The roses occupy a slender no-man's-land between the pasture grass encroaching from the orchard and the English ivy climbing up the roadcut and over the bank. They bloom and ramble year after year without much help from me. A layer of dead, wet maple leaves might at least knock back the grass. *Well, if you'd weeded those roses when you should have …*

Stop it.

I wheeled the leaves over and forked them around the canes. On the third or fourth trip I took a good look and saw that about a third of the canes were dead. So I abandoned the leaves and got to work with the pruning shears. The canes were thicker than my thumb and tough as bamboo. I sawed the pruners back and forth, worrying the dull jaws through the stalks until my arm ached. I should have gone and fetched the loppers, or a saw. *Now you're getting somewhere. This is looking all right.* The energy singing through my arm brought relief from the nagging voice. It felt so good that a few sore muscles seemed a small price to pay.

It took me two hours to finish. By then I felt sharp pains through my wrist, and my fingers were swollen and sore. I should have known better, but I couldn't stop until I'd finished moving the leaves. Then I went inside and made myself a cup of tea. My wrist was killing me, but the chattering had subsided, and I was feeling much better. How odd that hard work should be both a hurting and a healing thing.

In the middle of the night I woke up with an aching forearm and numb fingers. I went to the kitchen and took two aspirins and found the home health book, which advised a hot compress or an ice pack, either one. "Experiment," it said, not very helpfully. I wrapped a heating pad around my wrist—unable to bear the thought of an ice pack against my tender bones—and got a fitful few hours' sleep.

I spent the next day wearing a wrist brace on my right arm, and also an elastic bandage around my left forearm, against the chronic tendinitis in my elbow, which seemed to get worse all of a sudden. Awkwardly bandaged, I struggled to do the simplest things—turn a doorknob, squeeze a toothpaste tube, open a can. I felt myself hunker down, move gingerly; I couldn't afford careless or extravagant gestures. I anticipated pain, winced before I even felt anything.

I tried to be a good sport, but I felt outrage: I don't deserve this! I was touchy and distracted, and beneath the irritation was fear. I need my strong arms to get things done. Everywhere I looked I saw things to do, urgent things to do. What if I can't do them? If my arms are too weak to embrace this home and nurture it, what will hold it together?

John says, "Let me do it."

But that's not the point, I thought.

Then what is the point?

I don't know.

I woke up the next night and couldn't feel my hand. I padded into the bathroom and took two aspirins. Then I lay and stared at the ceiling, trying to ball my fist.

What is the point?

I don't know.

What are you doing? The voice inside had lost its sharpness. Outside the rain came down. *What am I doing?*

I don't know.

What am I doing?

This must be about more than pruning roses, more than a tidy garden. I can't feel my hand, but I can feel my insides, and they hurt.

There is so much anger inside me, so much fear. The voice was gentle. *What is it? Why do I have to keep going until I hurt myself?*

Sometimes this place feels like a tyrannical parent. I try so hard to appease the anger, meet the endless demands, and when the smiles come, they're so rare and so precious and they feel so good that I work even harder, trying to keep them coming.

Hmm.

Am I trying to please Mommy? The Mommy from a long time ago that I carry around inside my head?

Hmm. Maybe.

Or maybe this is about trying to fix my dad. Cleaning up the sloppy places, worrying off the old dead stems. Being a good daughter.

That was a long time ago.

But if I'd just tried harder, been a better kid …

That's not true. And it's too late anyway.

Or maybe it's because I know I couldn't fix my dad, but I can by god fix this place.

Maybe that's it.

But I can't fix this place; it's too much for me. And even if I could make it perfect, what difference would it make now? Watever is driving me, I want it to stop. *It's over and done. Let go of it.*

But what if this place falls apart?

It won't fall apart. It will always be a mess one way or another. It is what it is.

I can't let go of it. Something bad will happen to me.

Nothing bad will happen. Love this place or hate it. Stay here or leave. It is what it is. It is not what holds me together.

Then what does?

Something bigger than a tumble-down old schoolhouse on three weedy acres.

I'm not so sure about that.

Trust me.

Lying there with crippled arms, cocooned in a heating pad, waiting for the aspirin to work, I felt as helpless as I ever had.

The next Saturday, the weather was cloudy and cool but dry. My arms felt better, and I was severely tempted to get out with pruners and weeding tools. I talked myself out of it, but I still couldn't stay away from the housework. Sweeping the basement— my wrist still hurt a little—I remembered the clouds of dust I used to raise in the early days. I've worn down more than a few brooms on that rough concrete floor. Years of sweeping have scoured out the fissures, polished the ridges and swirls, and every time I sweep there is a little less dirt in the dustpan. Maybe I am gaining on this place.

Later I went outside and gathered up the plastic buckets scattered around the orchard. I braced myself for the nagging voice, expecting a scolding for leaving them out all these weeks, but the voice was quiet today. I hosed out the buckets and carried them to Grandma's old chicken house. As I pushed open the creaky door and saw the mess of irrigation hose and plastic-webbed folding chairs and handleless garden tools and old tomato cages woven with brown tendrils, I felt the familiar disquiet: *Oh, no, another mess!* But I took a deep breath and shoved the hose aside with my foot and cleared a square-foot space and stacked the buckets there. Then I pulled the door closed till it latched, hearing it scrape across the plywood threshold like a sticky windshield wiper. No need to open this door again till next spring.

Spring Planting

⧼⧽

The seeds I planted in the mud this spring are sprouting: chard, lettuce, parsley. It's been a long, wet winter here along the Little Lucky, and my heart bounces when I see the green tips of romaine spears uncurling, delicately rimed with mud. The gloomy Oregon winter almost makes me forget spring will come again. I'm glad the earth remembers. The tulips my mother brought me last Easter, stuck hastily in the ground and forgotten, have come to life again. I see their pink cups bobbing amid the leggy Oregon-grape stalks out in the side yard.

I am a slow learner about gardens. When we moved here I knew little about growing things: plants, soils, mulch, nitrogen, compost, all the rest of it. I was a long time learning even the basics: when to plant, when to prune, which plants need sunshine and which need shade. We were young, with high ideals and fuzzy objectives, green as grass, yearning to get closer to the land, here on Grandpa's little farm. We waved our hands expansively over our domain. We'll make it work somehow.

Somehow, we did, although it took many lessons, painful and funny and both. The goats that ate us out of house and home and gave us only a dribble of milk, which Gavin and Mary wouldn't touch. The piglets that escaped under the fence and trotted up to the neighbors. The rampant Himalaya blackberry vines that curl around my arms and rip my flesh and make me curse the ground like God after Adam's fall. The clayey Willamette Valley soil in mid-August, baked hard as a roasting pan.

I remember talking to a neighbor during those hard first years. She and her husband owned a blueberry farm, and I mentioned that we had blueberries, too, but they weren't doing very well. I must have looked like the greenhorn I was, for she said (with the air of someone teaching a kindergartner how to tie his shoes), "Well, you have to feed them, and water them, and prune them."

Prune them? Oh. How do you do that?

She spread her hands helplessly.

Fortunately, a garden can give you feedback in a year or less. Even a slow learner like me can eventually catch on. And sometimes, through luck or grace, you reap what you don't sow, like my mother's pink Easter tulips, or the tough little roses my grandmother put in three decades ago, which have responded to my sporadic weeding and watering with a gift of bloom.

Now I have learned how to prune blueberries. I know you can stick a cut-off grapevine into the ground and it will leaf out and make a new plant. I remember which things need sun and which need shade, and (mostly) when to feed the roses.

Gavin came home from the university the other day and told us he wanted to transfer to another college and study to be an architect.

Learning to negotiate the first few years of college is a lot like learning to grow a garden. The feedback is pretty immediate, the stakes are relatively low, and you learn first of all what doesn't work. In two years Gavin has learned that he does not want to study engineering, computer science, Japanese, business, political science, or history. But each wrong choice got him closer to the right one, or what seems like the right one now—another thing about learning is you're never sure when you're done.

His father and I worry about this choice, just as we'd worried about all the others. It's going to take another three years, maybe four—can he stay the course? And what about job prospects? Will he make enough money to cover his loan payments? All the parental concerns, which Gavin waved aside with an expansive hand. He will make it work, he says.

When you raise a garden, there are many chances to learn from your mistakes. Not so when you raise children. There's only one feedback loop, or maybe only part of one, a single, lazy lariat arcing around you from all the times you hug your boy when he's crying, and from all the times you do something unforgivable and then have to face him, have to look into his woeful, wise, ancient eyes. One lazy loop, and by the time it catches you and tugs you forward, it's too late—he's gone, off to study architecture in Portland or journalism in Canada or throat-singing in Tuva, to do his own thing, live his own life.

How do you know when you've learned? How do you know when you've failed? Here is an axiom: It's when the stakes are highest that the feedback is slowest. It's when you have the most to lose that the lessons are agonizingly obscure.

"Okay, honey," we told him. "You do what you feel is best." For us, so far, this has been a forgiving universe. I pray the same for him.

Fiery Blood

❧❧

My daughter played for Central High in the state girls' basketball championship. Mary was a senior and a starting post. She's a middling shooter, reliable at the line, and a competent defender. At five feet eleven and one hundred sixty-five pounds, she was an intimidating presence on the court.

A basketball game is a contest of muscle and bone, elemental as a catfight, yet leashed with conventions and taboos—no eye-gouging, no fingers around the neck, drop everything when the ref whistles. A basketball game arouses and discharges atavistic passions. At home my daughter talks politics, plays the piano, naps with her cat, reads Jonathan Swift, does differential calculus. She flies to the defense of the downtrodden, and she tells corny jokes. She's at ease with her peers and with grownups, both. She is thoroughly civilized.

On the court she is pushy, tough, crafty, obnoxious, brave, blindly partisan, consumingly loyal. She endures pain. Her adversaries fear her, and her teammates love her with a love beyond reason, a tribal loyalty baptized in adrenalin and sealed in sweat. Where did she get this? I ask myself. Not from me, or her dad—it was not a gift we had to give.

Indeed, she is giving it to us, extending us membership in this community of ritual violence. I join the other parents in the stands, the faceless fans, the rooters. I feel myself drawn in almost against my will, sucked into the maelstrom of emotion, resisting it yet craving it. We yell, we gesticulate with our popcorn boxes. We are rapt, panting, beside ourselves, prisoners of the moment. "Hey REF," we scream. "Whyncha get in the GAME, REF? Whyncha get some new GLASSES, REF?" "Come on, baby baby," we moan. "Come on, baby, just shoot the ball." "DE-fense," we incant, a hoarse supplication. "DE-fense. DE-fense. DE-fense."

The girls started the season with a new coach and a new playbook, and things looked pretty shaky at first. They played last year's reigning champions in a preseason game, a team from a private prep school in Eugene with a reputation for a ferocious offense and habitual discreet fouling. This team lived up to its reputation, beating our girls by twenty-two points.

The defeat jumpstarted them. The girls grieved for a couple of days, and then they went to work, learning the new coach's offense and beefing up their defensive strategies. They perfected lightning-like passes—a glance over one shoulder and a quick, blind chest pass in the opposite direction, or a deft bounce from the wing to the post for an easy lay-in. Mary got so she could feint a shot, duck as her opponent went up to block, and then spring up like a lioness and bury the ball in the net.

They won the season opener and kept on winning. They beat their league archrivals three times—the same team that had flattened them three times last year before taking second place at the championship. Midway through the season our girls knew they were headed for State. They were beating the other league teams in a walk. Rival coaches could be spotted in the stands at every game, scribbling furiously. The sports pundits at the newspapers started ranking them—sixth in the state 3A division, then fourth, then third, then second. First-ranked was the Eugene team that had beaten them so badly in preseason play.

The state tournament was held in a cavernous domed stadium, a giant Quonset hut with klieg lights. The brightness, the people-noise, the overheated sweaty air, the blaring of pep bands, and the pervasive odor of popcorn made an irresistible barrage of stimuli. The girls first stomped a team from a small school in the southern part of the state. That was a piece of cake, but the next team was not so easy. They were from Madras, a tough blue-collar town east of the mountains. Their star players were sisters from one of the Warm Springs tribes, the younger a point guard, the elder a center. These girls were athletic and aggressive, and their teamwork, with each other and with the rest of the team, was beautiful to watch, a strenuous ballet.

The fans were in an agony of excitement, standing, sitting, jumping up again. Whistles pierced the air, and the girls' feet thundered on the hardwood. The pep band shook the bleachers. A plump man with a blond stubbly crew cut and a voice like a chain saw, seated with the Madras fans, shouted "Travel!" every time our team had possession. "Travel! Travel!" he snarled, again and again. Another man down the row yelled, "Hey! Don't let her pick your pocket! Watch your butt!" A half-grown boy beside him echoed in a quavery tenor, "Yeah! Watch your butt!"

The gym got warmer, noisier. A couple of the parents (ours or theirs I don't know), incensed by the refereeing, exploded: "Hey, ZEBRA! Where's the foul, ZEBRA! Over the back!" The girls galloped up and down, followed by the referees in their black and white stripes. The whistle screamed. The gym was an ocean of noise. The referees' faces shone with sweat. The girls dripped sweat down the sides of their jerseys. "Travel!" snarled the crew-cut man when Mary had the ball. "She did NOT travel," I shouted back at him. The whistle screamed; foul on Madras. "Old stupid-head, old stupid-head," bleated the boy, suddenly soprano. "Travel!" moaned the crew-cut man, holding his head in his hands.

The game was a bruising war of attrition. Our girls won by a single point, a free throw sunk in the last few seconds.

It is delicious and dangerous, this dissolving of self into fan. We share occult phrases, incantations. " .... gotta get those boards .... nothin' but net .... airball! airball! .... shut her down!" We sound alike, look alike, screw up our faces identically when we yell. In real life we are Gail and John, César and Eulalia, Judy and Fred; we are the schoolteacher and the software engineer, the art historian, the police chief. At the basketball tournament, none of that matters. At the tournament we are only We, the Fans, the Team, the Panthers, Big Red. We bask in the moist bond, glad to be rid of our worldly burdens. We hug and high-five, and we lift our hands to heaven.

The final game was against the Eugene team, last year's champs. We resented this team because, being a private-school team, they can draw their players from anyplace. "They *recruit*," we murmured to one another, in the same tone in which we might say, "They eat babies for breakfast." Besides, they're too damned cocky. Being a fan nourishes such resentments. We develop a keen sense of injustice, carry a chip on our shoulder; we're always the underdogs, and the refs are always out to get us.

Early in the first quarter the Eugene post kneed Mary hard but unobtrusively in the ribs. She was a tall, pretty girl with a mop of curly ponytail, and I detected a distinct on-purpose pout to her mouth as she collided with my daughter. No foul was called, even though Mary winced, doubled over, and limped off the floor. That got my blood up. "Did you see that?" I shouted to John. "She tried to take her out. Hey, ref! Intentional foul!" But the referee paid no attention. The coach benched Mary till she caught her breath—a few minutes only—and then sent her back in.

Our girls played a brilliant game. After Eugene sank the first field goal, we surged ahead and kept the lead until the end. Unused to playing catch-up, the Eugene girls were fatally rattled, and we beat them by five points. It was a sweet, sweet victory, all the more delicious because the Eugene team had been so sure they were unbeatable.

The next day, reading the sports page, I saw a photo of the Eugene girls hugging and crying. I felt a hot trickle of shame. I had rejoiced at their suffering. I had laughed at the agony of young girls, not enemies or ogres, just high-school girls like my own daughter.

I was feeling jumpy and unsettled anyway, kind of hung-over, as if I had overindulged the night before. As if I'd made a fool of myself at a party, dancing on the table, letting the intoxication wash through me and dissolve every shred of reason and decency, set loose those mischievous passions.

The Red Dress

The first thing I have to do, before I start talking about women and power and choices, is to tell you about the red dress. The dress is a clingy sheath of knit jersey and Spandex, candy-apple red, shot through with silver threads that catch and scatter light like a spinning mirrored ball. It has a generous slit up the back seam to show off smooth and shapely legs. My daughter wore the dress to her high school winter formal dance, the Sno-Ball. Mary stood six feet two in strappy open-toed sandals with three-inch heels, and her toenails were painted red to match the dress. She wore a silver brocade bandeau in her blond hair, and her hair was a corona that captured and deflected all the light in the universe onto her glowing face.

Her regal beauty stunned me. Looking at her was like looking at a supernova, glories streaming from afar. I could hardly believe this was the same girl I have seen a hundred times in sweaty jersey and slumped ponytail, wresting a basketball from an opponent's hands with a savage yank and sinking a perfect lay-in, the same girl I have heard defending her opinions against a roomful of adversaries, passionate, cogent, fearless.

There is power in being a beautiful woman, and doubled power in knowing you are a beautiful woman. It's not just the luck of being born with pleasing facial features; that's necessary, but it's not sufficient. Carriage counts for a lot, and so does dignity, confidence, irony, cool control, meaningful glances, measured smiles and frowns. All these things give a beautiful woman power to sway men's thoughts and impulses, and to grind plain women down with envy.

I used to think beauty was a one-dimensional sort of power. (That is, if beauty is a choice and not just an accident; I was never entirely sure about that.) The beauty of a beautiful woman, I thought, always depends on the esteem of others; her beauty is always defined by someone or something else; it can be granted or taken away without her permission. Besides, beauty has an opportunity cost, or so I told myself. A woman can't be beautiful and also zany, or loopy, or ballsy, or funny, or radical, or gross, or intellectual.

So if a woman chooses beauty, I told myself (if it is a choice and not an accident), then she forgoes real power, the power to decide for herself what kind of person she will become, the power to measure her accomplishments by her own yardstick. A simple tradeoff: beauty for power, power for beauty, but you can't have both.

And so, acting as if it were a choice (of course, for me it could have been a virtue-of-necessity kind of thing), I chose to wear calf-length dark skirts, flat shoes, earth-toned jackets, button earrings, and plainly dressed hair. I did it because there are higher things in life (I told myself) than mere beauty. Of course I had doubts and fears about my looks—who doesn't?—and I coped with them by telling myself, *You look just fine, and now stop thinking about how you look.* Even now, to mention beauty in a sentence that also contains the pronoun "I" makes me feel a little squirmy, as if I've broken some rule of etiquette or good taste.

When my sister Leslie's children were small, a friend of mine remarked that of her two girls, the eldest, then five, "was going to be a beauty." She said this in front of both girls. Well, of course she is, I thought. Leslie was always the cute one (everybody said so when we were young); it makes sense that her girls would be pretty, too. But it hurt me that someone would carelessly tell one sister that she was prettier than the other. They were young, but not too young to get the message.

My own grasp on beauty is tenuous, easily lost. A blue mood can take it away, or a too-tight waistband, or an irritable or distracted remark from my husband. Beauty is a preoccupation I wish I didn't have, and I didn't want to wish it on my daughter. I didn't want her to chase after false gods. I wanted her to grow up to be a woman, not a lady or a babe but a complex, feisty, loving, true-to-herself female human being.

❧❧

Then I saw her in the red dress, and all my old notions scattered like birds. What if my idea of beauty was too narrow? What if beauty really is more than skin-deep? What if it's something you gather in from outside and weave into the fabric of your soul like a bright silver thread, making it your own, so that nobody can take it away? What if it starts with the admiration of others but doesn't end there? What if it adds to, rather than subtracts from, a woman's repertoire of power? What if you don't have to make a choice? What if you can be a babe, a lady, and a woman, all at once?

My daughter seems to feel free to be all these things; she senses no contradictions. She is, in fact, becoming the woman I always wanted her to be. She is growing into her own womanhood by opening a door that, whether by choice or accident, was not available to me. I'm glad she found it. Maybe it's not too late for me.

My Mother's Wedding

～～

After living alone for thirty-six years, my mother got remarried. The way it happened would make a romantic movie. There was a fifty-fifth high school reunion in Iowa City, and Marvin, who lives in northern Minnesota, called all his surviving classmates and invited them to come. My mother told him she was planning to fly from Portland to Minneapolis and rent a car at the airport. Well, said Marvin, why didn't he just pick her up instead and they would drive down together? They followed the Mississippi south in the August heat, and somewhere on the way they fell in love.

I'll bet he remembered her when he picked up the phone to call her, a pretty, scholarly girl with a wide smile, a singer and a pianist. In their senior year they'd sung in *Iolanthe,* the Gilbert and Sullivan operetta, he in the lead, she in the chorus. I'm not sure she remembered him. She was one of those girls who was beautiful but didn't know it. I remember a picture of her in a 1950 University of Oregon yearbook. The picture shows Mom as a Junior Weekend princess, wearing a strapless formal and long gloves and waving from a convertible. "I was completely surprised when I was chosen," she told me when I asked her about the photo. At the time I didn't believe her—I was an awkward, pimply, too-big teenager. But now I do. She is still beautiful, and she still seems not to know it, or care. At seventy-three, she has the vigor of a woman in her fifties. She has good bones and an electric smile. Her hair is silver and her eyes are dark, with radiating laugh lines. She doesn't fuss about her looks. She goes out to breakfast in a jogging suit, wearing a touch of lipstick. She plays the Liebeslieder Walzes with her sister Ann at the piano, frowning and squinting at the music through her bifocals, and then throwing back her head and laughing when she makes a mistake.

I am not sure, but I think my father may have been driving the convertible in the picture. She'd met him in her sophomore year at college. He was her roommate Eunice's brother, an up-and-coming timber entrepreneur from Coos Bay, good-looking and fond of flashy cars. They fell in love. He was married, not happily. She took a summer job at Mount Rainier, and he drove up every weekend to see her. His divorce came final, and they got engaged. Then he broke it off; he wasn't ready, he said; he wanted to try one last time to make it up with his wife. "I think Onie still loves me," he told her. But maybe she didn't, or maybe it didn't matter by then, because he came back. They were married in this house on Elkins Road on April 7, 1951. It was a small wedding, just family and a few friends. I've seen the picture, Mom coming down the stairs in her long dress, dark hair shining against her veil.

We met Marvin in September, a month after the reunion. I was having a family picnic and she asked if she could bring a friend. When I saw the way he looked at her I knew something was up, but my mother said nothing. She introduced him as "my friend Marvin." Marvin is not much like my father in looks—he is shorter, rounder, nice-enough-looking but not handsome. From his conversation at the picnic we learned some facts: he was widowed after forty-nine years of marriage, has two children and three grandchildren, lives on a lake in Minnesota so pure you can drink out of it, waded ashore at Utah Beach when he was seventeen. I was not sure what to make of him. His eyes followed my mother around, but if she noticed she didn't show it. He talked a lot, and mostly seemed to know what he was talking about. He told Sven-and-Ole jokes in dialect, and he made the occasional ribald remark in his broad Midwestern accent. Marvin and my dad had one thing in common: my mother always liked a good storyteller.

Two months later Marvin wrote us a letter. *Your mother and I are in love and we have decided to get married,* he wrote. *Many people our age would simply move in together, but that's not what I want, and I don't think it's what your mother wants, either. We hope you will give us your blessing.* My mother had not said a word to me. I called her, a little miffed. Why didn't you tell me? I wanted to say. "What's going on?" I asked, then added, "Just so you know, I'm tickled to death." "So am I," she said.

Our family spent the last years of Mom's and Dad's marriage in Ukiah, California. Dad was trying desperately to hold himself together, trying to keep his job at the truck dealership, trying to keep his life from unraveling. To supplement his erratic income, Mom got a job at a state mental hospital a few miles from town. There she learned enough about social work to know she liked it. After the divorce, she made up her mind to move us four girls back to Oregon. She applied to the social work program at Portland State College and was offered a small fellowship. It would be enough, she hoped, to support us until she finished grad school and got on her feet.

The state hospital was the same one my father had entered a few months before the divorce, finally convinced that drink had gotten the better of him. "He was a model patient," my mother told me. "He memorized the Twelve Steps, he led the meetings, he shared his story from his heart." Released, sober and full of confidence, he found a job that took him to San Francisco on sales calls.

One day he walked into a bar and said, "Honey, bring me a double martini," and he was off. He didn't come home for three weeks. Uncle Ken went looking for him and found him holed up in a room somewhere. When he dried out enough to carry on a conversation, my mother asked him why. What do you say to someone who just doesn't come home? She wasn't accusing him or threatening him—she was beyond that, she said. "I just want to know why. What makes a happily sober man walk into a bar he's passed a dozen times before?"

Dad shook his head. "Virginia," he said, "if I had a clue myself, you know I'd tell you."

When Mom moved us north after the divorce, we landed in Vancouver, Washington, where my uncle Ralph helped us get settled. She enrolled in her master's program, and I started my junior year at Fort Vancouver High School. Mom's fellowship covered her tuition and school expenses, but there wasn't much left over for groceries and gas and clothes, let alone vacations and Christmas.

Dad was in tough shape. He'd gone back to Coos Bay and was living in a shabby house with Eileen, a kind and competent nurse who, out of who knows what impulse of compassion, took him in, cared for him, drank with him, picked up after him. He wasn't much help to us.

I sewed jumpers and skirts for myself and pajamas for my sisters. I got an after-school job at a day-care center, playing the piano and teaching four-year-olds to sing "Que Sera Sera." I cooked dinner: meat loaf, spaghetti, macaroni and cheese, beans and wienies. I looked after my sisters when Mom had to study late. We took turns cleaning and doing dishes. We took care of each other, and we took care of Mom.

For Christmas Grandpa gave us a brand-new 1969 Volkswagen Beetle. When Mom saw it in the driveway, she cried. It was my job to drive my sisters to their various appointments, and one day, backing out of a slot in the doctor's office parking lot, I hooked a rear wheelwell on another car's bumper and dug a big vertical gash in the new Volkswagen. Cowed by the thought of the scolding I would get, I couldn't bring myself to tell her. Two weeks went by, three weeks, and she didn't mention it. I was starting to relax. Then one evening, she came into Melinda's and my room, sat on my bed, gave me a tender look, and said, "Gail, do you know anything about that gash in the car?" I had feared her anger, but her compassion undid me, and I sobbed out my confession. She forgave me, of course, and we hugged and cried for a few minutes. Not long after that, she got her master's degree, and I graduated from high school.

My mother didn't have much idea of how to plan a wedding. My sister Leslie and I talked her through her early jitters—what about a cake? What about flowers? What should we all wear? Leslie, a born executive, mapped it all out and assigned us our tasks. She and Mom would sew their own dresses. I was going to sew mine, too, but then I found a green silk dress with spaghetti straps, far too expensive. "Buy it," my mother told me impulsively; then, as her frugality kicked in, she said, "I'll pay half." Auntie Ann lined up a string quartet with herself on the cello to play Pachelbel's *Canon* at the wedding and "The Nearness of You" at the reception. I bought lemonade and raspberry sherbet for the punch. My sisters Laurie and Leslie and my daughter Mary and I practiced "Be Thou My Vision" in four-part harmony.

The morning of the wedding, Leslie and I and our husbands and five of our children—all four of hers, plus my Mary—stuffed ourselves into Mom's little apartment in Salem to get ready. We girls and women jostled one another in the upstairs bedroom, pulling on bras and slips and pantyhose. Downstairs, sixteen-year-old Elliot and eight-year-old Luke looked solemnly handsome in their dark suits. Emily and Lindsey, fourteen and twelve, wriggled awkwardly into their sheaths and teetered on their new high heels. They were coltish, more girl than woman, and they walked like the athletes they were. It didn't take Lindsey five minutes to rip out the kickpleat in the back of her dress. The two of them crammed themselves into the guest bathroom to apply their makeup, an interesting novelty for them. They shouted out old songs: "R-E-S-P-E-C-T! Tell you what it means to me!" They curled their hair with slender curling irons and filled the air with a fog of hairspray.

Leslie was in the upstairs bathroom with Mom, helping her choose the exact right shade of lipstick. At my mother's throat was a rhinestone collar my father had given her before I was born. In her silver-streaked hair she wore a slim rhinestone tiara. In her mineral-blue dress she seemed to glow with a dark fire. She looked splendid and forbidding; her radiance seemed to warn against getting too close. But Leslie held Mom's chin in her left hand and carefully brushed lipstick on her lips. Their faces were two inches apart. I stood back, as if watching a love scene in a movie, feeling my heart tug toward her, unable to move.

⁓⁓

After she divorced Dad, Mom let a lot of time go by before she began to date. I was upset when she did. I didn't think any of the men she dated were worthy of her. There was Milo, wry and scholarly, who collected rare books and gave us a first edition of *Alice's Adventures in Wonderland.* There was Bill, big and boisterous, who collected antique wineglasses. I didn't like him touching her, hugging her around the waist; it made me feel sticky and shivery. Then there was another guy—I have to dig for his name. Wilbur. An earnest divorced stockbrroker raising three snotty children who took me out to breakfast one time and asked me miserably why my mother wouldn't marry him. *Because you're pitiful,* I didn't answer.

When she was out with one of them, I would lie sleepless, wondering what they were doing, when she was coming home. I was afraid she would fall in love with some stranger and leave us. One night she came home in gay spirits, a little drunk, and I lashed into her. I had no business doing it, but I was so angry, so scared, I couldn't stop myself. I was crying, and shouting I don't know what. She shouted back at me: "You shut up! I have a right to have a little fun! You don't know what it's like!" We flew at each other's hearts like confused birds, and each of us left a bruise.

We climbed gingerly into our cars and drove to St. Timothy's for the wedding. I had the sherbet and soda pop in a box in the backseat. Leslie detoured south to pick up Melinda. "Will you take me home when I want to go home?" Melinda asked Leslie.

"Yes, Melinda, I will," said Leslie.

"Gail, if she doesn't take me home, will you take me home?"

"Yes, Melinda, I will. Don't worry."

St. Tim's is a "high" church, meaning there are embroidered vestments and incense and candles and pealing organ music. Father Rick is about half Mom's age and has known her for years; she's been a pillar of good works at that church. He was clearly tickled at this turn of events in her life. He broke into chuckles at

various points in the rehearsal, especially when he spoke the prayer
that the couple, if it be God's will, receive the gift of children.

My sisters and I walked Mom down the aisle, Laurie and I in
front, Leslie and Melinda behind, and our mother in the middle,
as if we carried her in a litter. When Father Rick asked, "Who gives
this woman to be married to this man?" we said in unison, "We
do!" The congregation laughed softly. Then my sisters sat down
with their families and I stood alone with my mother. Marvin
stood across the aisle with his best man. He and my mother held
hands, right hand to right hand, and my stomach felt a little
squeeze. Her voice shook a little, and Marvin's did, too, when
they recited their vows.

When Father Rick said, "I pronounce you husband and wife,"
my mother left my side and crossed the aisle and stood next to
her husband.

Wait a minute, I thought. *Where are you going?* I stood there
awkwardly, feeling the empty space beside me. She was leaving
me, going to someone else. Would he take good care of her?

Had I taken good care of her?

Was that my job, to take care of her?

Whether yes or no, it was done now. The role or mission or
burden of the eldest daughter, that vocation assumed or given or
imagined early in life, that job was done. Well or poorly, gladly
or resentfully, deftly or awkwardly, for better or for worse, it is
done.

Starlings

First it was the streaks of birdlime down the side of the house, and then it was the raspy chirruping under the eaves. The starlings had moved in. Last summer, after we'd finished putting on the new roof, we carelessly skipped the final chore of nailing the soffit boards under the eaves, leaving openings where birds, mice, bugs, and any other crawling or flying creatures could come and go at will. So it had to happen: give a starling a hole, any hole, and it will make a nest there.

The starling breeds everywhere, says our bird book: "in dovecotes, such church steeples as furnish safe nesting places, in holds and crevices about houses, in niches under the eaves, in electric light hoods, bird houses, nesting boxes, woodpecker holes, and hollow trees." It doesn't mind the close proximity of humans, being "a hardy, capable, and prolific bird" with many centuries of adaptation to human ways.

Our new tenants aren't scared of us at all. As I crouch in the front garden bed pulling weeds, the parent birds fly in and out of the holes with bits of food in their beaks, pausing every now and then to rasp furiously at me. There seem to be two families up there, or at least two nests: one just inside the opening above the front porch, and the other in the back corner above our bedroom. The babies wake us up in the morning with their monotonous *shreep shreep.* During the day, as the parents approach with beakfuls of food, the shreeping becomes higher-pitched and more demanding.

I feel a spark of kinship as I watch those starling parents strenuously feeding their babies. John and I were young parents when we moved into this protected cranny, this hole in the universe, this place we hadn't created. We spent most of our time and energy figuring out how to keep our babies fed and sheltered. Our children were the focal point of our lives, the motive for everything we did. It was a lot of work, but it was an unarguable imperative.

Sometimes, during the hard early years, I was afraid this nest we'd chosen was not warm enough or strong enough to nurture these children until they were ready to fly. Then I'd see Gavin cavorting across the backyard with a cape made from a bedsheet, declaiming Luke Skywalker's lines from *Star Wars.* I'd see Mary swinging high, pumping her legs vigorously and singing to herself. I'd see the two of them push our old tractor tire to the top of the hill and cram themselves inside it and roll down to the bottom, spinning themselves silly, and then push it back up and do it again.

They climbed into burlap feed bags and sack-raced each other down the front walk. They combed the woods for owl pellets and teased them apart to find the mummified bones of mice. Gavin made boats from styrofoam meat trays and toothpicks and sailed them on the neighbor's creek, and, when he was a little older, riddled them with BBs. Mary picked blackberries in the woods and came home with face and hands stained blue. No. This was a good nest.

Soon one of the starling nests is empty—no adult birds flying back and forth, no baby-noise coming from that part of the ceiling. So the little birds are gone, to fly or not, to survive or not. The parents are out of there: mission accomplished. You hear about parent birds pushing their babies out of the nest when instinct tells them it's time. I'm not sure humans have this same instinct, or if they do, it is vague and attenuated, weakened by conflicting, vestigial attachments. At least, that's the way it is for me. I hear about some people's grown children who move back in at age twenty-two or twenty-eight, kids who can't seem to find their wings. I don't want this to happen to us, and yet, now that our children are in their teens, I find myself wanting to delay the moment of flight. I have a hard time giving up that single-minded nurturing instinct even though the kids don't want it any more.

I do know our children need nurturing of another kind, the nurturing of friend to friend, of mentor to disciple, the tough tenderness of mature commitment in the face of youthful vulnerability, the love that says Go, be free, and I love you all the more for leaving me. But that kind of nurturing requires different emotional musculature. It requires detachment, respect, and a distancing impulse that does not come naturally to me.

An odd thing about having older children is that now it is they who bring us food—not literal food, of course, but sustenance in the form of news about themselves and their lives, foreshadowings of the adults they are becoming. A dangerously large share of John's and my conversation is devoted to our children's school grades, their summer job prospects, their softball and basketball tournaments, their girl- and boyfriends, their social circles, their inner fears and fantasies, their dreams for the future; along with the benign or malevolent influences of the television and movies they watch, the music they listen to, and the friends they hang out with. Our children bring us this food, and we feast on it. What will we do when they bring it no longer? What will we do when they fly away?

On Mother's Day I went hiking up in the Cascades with friends—no children along, for once. Driving home, wonderfully tired, I pulled into the driveway and saw my son's precious vintage Mustang with the passenger's side bashed in and the headlight socket pointed crazily skyward. "Oh, my god!" I screamed, stopping the car with a lurch. "Ohmygodohmygod!"

At that moment the front door of the house opened and Gavin came down the steps. He was fine. "Oh thank you thank you," I sobbed and flung my arms around him. He extricated himself with dignity and told me what had happened. A woman on her way to deliver a casserole to a bereaved family, herself distracted with grief perhaps, had made a U-turn right in front of him without looking. "She admitted it was her fault, and her insurance is going to pay for it," said Gavin. "They'd better give me enough to fix my car, that's all I have to say."

The car had come to us three years before, with a beat-up body and a tired but functioning engine. It cost seven hundred dollars. John and Gavin pounded out the dents, puttied and sanded the body, and painted it themselves, a vivid electric blue. They pulled the engine, a two-hundred, and installed a more-powerful two-eighty-nine which they'd had to overhaul first. At Gavin's insistence they'd put in a four-barrel carburetor—John didn't approve because it made the car surge like a jackrabbit, but he'd assented after subjecting his son to dark warnings about what happened to boys who got careless with squirrely cars. The restoration had taken countless hours and had cost much more than the initial investment. The Mustang was more than a car; it was the emblem of a father's and a son's steadfast nurturing of each other. My most enduring memory of that car is the image of two sets of feet sticking out from under it, both of them belonging to grown men, and Gavin's are bigger than his father's.

The car wreck and its repercussions—talking with the insurance agent, totting up the damage, searching the ads for another car, finding a way to get Gavin to school and work while all this was being negotiated—consumed our attention for weeks. That along with Mary's successful softball tournament (the girls took second out of sixteen teams and Mary hit a triple and two doubles) has nourished our conversation long enough to distract us, at least for now, from the question of what on earth we are going to talk about when the kids are gone.

The Big Lucky

The flood was all over the TV. We saw people paddling canoes up Main Streets past car roofs sticking up out of the water, volunteer sandbaggers sweating in yellow rainsuits. We saw apartment houses riding mudslides like novice skiers, crashing at the bottom in a welter of splintered wood.

For us life seemed ordinary. I didn't feel that light-headed, time-is-standing-still feeling that comes when some sudden event lifts you out of your ordinary self. Others were surely feeling it, but the drama and horror of the flood came to me thirdhand. We did see some high water on Elkins Road. By Wednesday I could look across the fields to the south and see the Little Lucky's north bank crawling toward the back of the house. The creeks on either side of us swelled up. The one to the west overwhelmed its culvert and flowed over the road, while the one to the east took over the road's lower, banked edge, leaving one narrow lane bare for traffic.

The most bothersome thing for us was the groundwater that seeped into the basement. I spent most of Wednesday and Thursday vacuuming it up with a wet-and-dry vacuum. Except for a couple of hours Thursday morning, when the water came in faster than I could get it out, I pretty much kept on top of it. I had the TV on loud, to hear it (barely) over the vacuum. The stories that came onto the screen were dramatic, not like the petty inconveniences we were experiencing. Each one was a tragedy for someone. The eight-year-old girl who went to get the mail and drowned in a ditch. The family, homeless until weeks before the flood, who watched the Tualatin River flow through their new apartment. The man whose house tumbled into the Columbia with him in it, saved; his wife, who had just stepped across the threshold, headed for safety, lost. And, closer to home, the eighty-four-year-old woman who drowned in an overflowing slough of the Luckiamute River after her car was knocked off the road, her companion saved by a couple of teenaged boys in a dramatic rescue. To me these all seemed slightly unreal, like a made-for-TV movie.

≈≈

John and Mary and I sat down to supper on Wednesday night. The TV was stilled. Except for the hard rain outside it was a normal evening. Then we heard a car pull into the driveway, and I went out to see. It was Gavin's friend Greg and two of their fraternity brothers. "Can we come in?" Greg asked. "Gavin's right behind us. Don't worry—he's all right."

"Don't worry?" I echoed. Then another car pulled in, and Gavin climbed out, along with another knot of young men. His hair was soaked, and I saw water dripping from his jacket sleeves and his pant legs. "Hi, Mom," he said. "I'm okay. This is Tim."

Dazed, I said, "Hi, Tim," to a tall, husky young man who was also dripping wet. The boys trooped up the front steps and into the house. "I need some dry clothes," Gavin said. "And I need a Band-Aid. I cut my thumb. Does Dad have anything that would fit Tim? And can you wash these?"

"Tell me," I said.

They'd been on their way to an AC/DC concert in Portland. Driving north on Highway 99, they came to the Big Lucky bridge, about five miles from our house. Traffic was stopped; there'd been an accident. They saw a small car nose-down in the swollen slough. A man with a rope tied around his waist was standing thigh-deep a few feet out from the bank. The man was saying, "I can't make it, I can't make it."

Gavin looked at him, then took off his shoes and his jacket and plunged down the embankment into the water. Tim followed. The boys waded as far as they could, then swam the rest of the way to the sinking car. Gavin tried the driver's door. It was locked. Through the back window he could see two figures half-submerged.

Someone on the bank tossed Tim a hammer. Tim fumbled and almost dropped it, then made a quick cradle with his hands and recovered it before it sank. He handed the hammer to Gavin. Wrapping his legs around a tree, Gavin reared back and smacked the back windshield as hard as he could. It broke. He saw someone swimming up toward him from the passenger's side.

Gavin dropped the hammer inside the car and pulled away some of the broken glass with his hands, cutting his thumb. Then he reached in and grabbed a man by the armpits and hauled him halfway out. "You're going to have to help me," he told the man. "I can't do this all by myself; you're going to have to help me." He reached down and grabbed the man's knees and pulled them out. Then, gripping the man in a cross-chest carry, he swam over to Tim, who was treading water about five feet away. Together the boys dragged the man to shallow water. Others helped them pull him up onto the bank.

Gavin and Tim stayed with the man until the medics came, covering him with a blanket—he was shivering badly—and talking to him to keep him conscious. Some others immediately went back in to try to rescue the woman. But the car had sunk until only the tail end was sticking out of the water, and it was too late.

Gavin went downstairs to find some dry clothes for himself and Tim. The boys sat in the living room, a somber-looking bunch. They filled in a few more details, but nobody felt much like talking.

I was having a hard time, too. This flood was no longer at arm's length; this was no thirdhand story. My mind struggled with the shocking images. A car spinning off the road. A boy swimming in floodwater. A hammer smashing through glass. A man shivering for his life on a muddy riverbank. A woman strapped into a car seat, sinking in dark water; that was the worst.

After a while Gavin came upstairs wearing a faded shirt and too-tight jeans. He was fumbling with a Band-Aid. "All my good clothes are at school," he said. "Could you wash my jeans?"

I said, "Don't tell me you're still planning on going to that concert."

"Ah, Mom, it's okay," he said, hardly listening to himself, the words running together, *Ahmomitsokay*. The boys seemed glad to be on their way at last.

I washed the dishes after supper, trying to grasp Gavin's story, struggling with how fantastical it seemed. It pushed my ordinary reality into a remote corner of my mind: the spaghetti bowl on the table, the crumpled napkins, my hands in soapy water, all seemed unnecessary, like fantasies.

I became aware that this was a heroic deed, the kind of deed people get medals for, the kind recorded in ballads.

Then it occurred to me that Gavin's life might have been in danger; might still be in danger. What if he'd snagged his sleeve on the sinking car and gone down with it? What if he'd cut his wrist on the window glass, instead of his thumb? What if the man had struggled, pulling them both to the mucky bottom? What if the water was contaminated with some terrible germ or poisonous chemical?

I went to bed feeling proud, anxious, confused, scared. I slept fitfully, knowing the boys were still out and the water was rising.

The next day a woman called me on the phone. It was the daughter of the woman who had drowned. She had gone to look at the car and found the hammer inside, under the smashed back windshield. She got the story and Gavin's name from the sheriff.

She hoped Gavin didn't feel bad about not being able to save her mother, she said, weeping a little. "He did what he could. He saved a life. He should feel proud."

She offered to return the hammer. I told her it wasn't ours. I thought again of the hammer spinning through the dark into a boy's cold hands. Iron shattering glass. Solid illusion, unbelievable reality.

Legacy Structures

≋≋

Before we left for Scotland this June, I weeded the vineyard. The little naked sticks we stuck into the ground two winters ago are clothed with leaves, tender as kid leather, willow-green on their stems. The vineyard is small, only eighty-eight vines. I knew if I didn't get after the weeds now they'd be overtopping the vines by the time we got back.

So I got to work and dug out the quackgrass and thistles from around each vine. In the middle of the vineyard is a small Granny Smith apple tree we planted a few years ago, before we were thinking about grapes. We left it when we cleared the ground; we couldn't bear to take it out, not just yet. Some day it will have to go. But I enjoyed sitting in its dappled shade as I scrabbled in the dirt with my three-toed scratcher. As I worked, I hummed a song I'd learned in French class long ago: *Vive la vigne, la jolie jolie vigne* …. Long live the vine, the pretty, pretty vine.

Over at the end of the seventh row is the Winesap tree that John pruned hard ten years ago. It was one of Grandpa's full-size apple trees, and we wanted to bring it down to a manageable size. I was afraid the pruning had killed it, but it sprang back in full vigor the next spring, and now it's as big as it ever was.

We left quite a few vestiges of the old orchard when we put the grapes in. We didn't want to rip out or spray to death every stick and shred of vegetation; it didn't seem right. I don't mind using a little weed killer once in a while, but a broadcast of poison over the land seems extreme to me, literally overkill. So we cut down the oldest apple trees and piled them for firewood, and then scraped around their stumps with a tractor blade and called it good. A couple of the stumps are producing suckers, and growing between them are tall fescue and chickweed and the ubiquitous Himalaya blackberries, risen from the dead, bounding up from their immortal rhizomes. They like nothing so much as a good scalping.

We live with our history, here on the Little Lucky. We live with the shards and artifacts from Grandpa's time, and the time of the Elkins School before that, and the time of the donation-land-claim settlers before that, and the time of the Kalapuya before that. Old trees in the orchard, small glass bottles at the base of the foundation, faint stripes on the ground along the neighbor's fence where the railroad spur once ran.

At the forestry college where I work, they have a name for the fragments of old forest left on the land after logging. These are called "legacy structures": limbs and needles left to decay into humus, old fallen logs, stumps, and standing snags with rotten pockets for squirrels and birds to nest in. Like so much forestry lingo it's an awkward, abstracted phrase (consider "vegetation management," which means spraying the weeds with poison), but they had to come up with something to call the things that loggers are supposed to leave on the land.

Legacy structures represent a fairly recent development in forestry practice. A couple of decades ago loggers were supposed to sweep the forest floor clean like good housekeepers. In those days they Cat-skidded the discarded sticks and stumps into big piles and burned them. This they called "pumming"—"piling unmerchantable." Then the biologists discovered that forests need these pieces of decomposing wood and needle and weedy mat to keep themselves healthy. There has to be something left for the new forest to grow on.

When we moved here from Seattle twenty years ago, we had the notion that we were starting fresh, turning this old family place into our particular homeplace. We weren't wrong, exactly, but starting fresh is a complicated idea, or maybe it's a simple idea that turns complicated in the execution. John and I wanted to get out of the city, find a home in the country to raise our children. That was our stated intention, but beneath it was a yearning, I see now, to find a soft piece of ground that would accept our imprint as if we were the first humans there. We didn't know, then, that no place is ever new. Every place has legacy structures, some more obvious than others.

One of the first things we did was take out a row of Douglas firs across the front of the property, right underneath the power lines. Could have been Grandpa who planted them; could have been Bob, my mother's boyfriend for a while. The trees had been whacked off repeatedly by the power company's line crews until they resembled shaven hedges. Douglas firs are meant to grow tall and straight, and to deform them so grotesquely seemed wrong. Better to put them down.

The first spring after the Douglas firs were gone, wands of thorny stems emerged from the soil around their stumps. In June the wands bloomed, and I recognized my grandmother's climbing roses, ruffled buttons of flowers of the palest pink. I remembered them from when I was a little girl, how they lounged along the two-by-four fence that used to stand next to the road. The fence is gone now, its slabs rotted into the top of the roadcut. But every year the roses come out, looking for something to hold them up.

Our house, in the family for three generations, is a historical artifact in our part of the world. When we traveled to Scotland, I couldn't get over how old things are there. We saw the room in Edinburgh Castle where, more than four hundred years ago, Mary Queen of Scots had her baby, a little boy who grew up to be King James I of England. We saw the restored abbey on the island of Iona, where Saint Columba landed in 563, and we saw his Hill of the Abbot—"Torr an Aba"—the knoll of creased rock above the abbey, where the saint used to retreat to his writing hut. We saw an unearthed Roman fort near Hadrian's Wall, built about the time when the Jewish temple in Jerusalem was destroyed and the New Testament was beginning to be written down. We saw the ruins of a Stone Age village on the island of Orkney, little close-built dwellings with living rooms and storage shelves, sheltering families so long ago that I struggle to find something to compare it to. These people were raising their children in condominiums a thousand years before Abram came up out of Ur of the Chaldees.

We saw a red-sandstone church built a thousand years ago, with modern hymnals in the choir stalls. One hymnal had last week's Sunday bulletin protruding from the pages. I glanced at the list of hymns: *Jerusalem my happy home, when shall I come to thee?* I've sung that hymn in my own church.

We saw, in a pasture next to the train tracks, surrounded by grazing sheep, a ruined crofter's cottage, roof tiles scattered on the ground, stone walls standing jagged as battlements. A few hundred feet away was the "new" house, built some time in the last century.

The Scots are intimate with their history. Their land is a land of spareness and stones, while ours is a land of moisture and rot, a soft land that muffles the stories of those who were here eleven thousand years ago. And so we Johnny-come-latelies think we invented the place. A railroad track used to run across our fence line a few paces from where I was weeding the grapevines. Children living on farms farther up the Little Lucky used to ride the train to school here. There's no trace of the track now. Someone took the rails and ties away, and the grass pulled its shroud over the dead railroad, and trees grew up to bury the body. Now there's just the neighbor's barbed-wire fence.

In Scotland we learned about the homeless farmers who emigrated to Canada after the Highland Clearances of the eighteenth century. Living with your history can be a painful intimacy, especially if it's a history that others write and then foist upon you.

Yet even a land that oppresses must sometimes feel more hospitable than a land with nothing familiar to hold a person up. *By the waters of Babylon, there we sat down and wept. How shall we sing the Lord's song in a foreign land?* Is a fresh start even possible? These days America is full of Celtic bands, singing songs about when Allan a'Dale went a-hunting, and dark Molly of the glen, and follow me, my bonny lass, for I'll nae follow you. Wistfulness lives in the lyrics and the skirling harmonies, a legacy of transplantedness. Someone has said you can't go home again. What if you can't ever leave?

When we came back from Scotland, we saw our home with fresh eyes. The place looked scruffy. The house needed paint. The weeds were rampant. Kneeling and stooping, yanking pigweed from the ground with resentment-fueled energy, we talked about how tired we were of slaving over this place. We fantasized about finding a nice little quarter of an acre with nothing on it, or maybe just a house, a plain, new, well-built house, plumbing with no leaks and a roof with no holes and a foundation with no gaps. No memories, no baggage, no legacy structures. A fresh start, like the one we were looking for all those years ago.

It's late summer now, and the apples are beginning to swell on the Winesap tree. Ripe, the apples are tart and hard, not so good for eating but great for cidering. They make a cloudy, thick, russet juice that takes on a mild alcoholic tingle if you leave it in the refrigerator for a week. Last November we had the neighbors in for a cider pressing. We wheeled boxes of apples down from the orchard and cut and mashed and squeezed them until it got too cold. Then we went inside and had a party. We brought out the guitars and sang *Oh Shenandoah, I love your daughter.* We sang *My heart is down, my head is turning around, I had to leave a little girl in Kingston town.* Are there any songs in the world except songs about leaving home?

This place oppresses me, and it also holds me up. That's what makes it so hard. Watching my grandmother's roses come up year after year. Laughing with my friends, cramming apples into the grinder with sticky hands, bringing jugs of foaming juice to our lips. How can I bear to leave this? How can I sing my song in a foreign land?

Edges and Boundaries

≈≈

Friday, 4 a.m. We are driving up the Columbia Gorge through warm predawn darkness, into the rising sun. Mary has to be in Walla Walla by nine o'clock to move into her dorm, and it's a six-hour drive. This morning the Milky Way slants across the Columbia River, northeast to southwest. As it fades, the outlines of the basalt cliffs on the Washington side begin to surface out of the dark. Their faces are opaque, and the river is only a shade lighter. Starlight dances on the charcoal water for an instant, then sinks. The canyon is flooding with light—flooding like a real flood, as if the light were rising from beneath us. It's a change so gradual that the mind hardly registers it. It's like when you go outside to watch stars at night, and it takes a while for the dark to soothe your light-seared retinas. Then your eyes receive a glimmer, then another, and pretty soon the gauzy band of the Milky Way is so obvious, so splendid, you wonder how you couldn't see it before.

5:20 a.m. The river becomes translucent, like an ink wash on stippled paper. The basalt columns reveal their crooked plumb lines. The light foreshortens the perspective, making the canyon look like one in a Viewmaster slide.

6:10 a.m. The rising flood of daylight moves things around, spreads them out. There's movement on the inky surface of the river. The current curves around the hulk of The Dalles Dam, looming out of the water like a rectilinear island. It's light enough to read a map. On the radio they're playing the old song, "When I'm far away from you, my baby … The darkest hour is just before dawn." But that can't be true, I tell myself. It's been getting lighter for hours, and I still don't see the sun. When does dawn happen, anyway?

7:45 a.m. We have passed The Dalles and are approaching Biggs. We're in the high Central Oregon desert, but I don't know when we got here. A while ago there were dark Douglas firs bulked against the darker canyon walls. Then there were tumbled hummocks of rock and small sparse pines in shades of gray, and now I see dull-gold grass, rock, and rolling yellow prairie. The transition is so thorough, so immense, it's hard to believe it happened. I look behind me at the freeway stretching westward. Where was the boundary line? There ought to be a way to know when you leave a familiar landscape and enter an unfamiliar one. It shouldn't take you by surprise like this.

8:41 a.m. We're almost to Pendleton. The edge of flame at the southeast horizon becomes a line, then a ball. The rays come straight on through the windshield. I flip my visor down and swallow the last of my cold coffee.

Saturday, 9 a.m. We are gathered in the auditorium for the convocation ceremony, a ritual as focused and intentional as any church service I'd ever been to, and with the same anchoring elements: Bach on the organ, a protocol for standing and sitting, homilies about honor and duty and destiny.

I managed to stay dry-eyed through all the business of installing Mary in her dorm room, in a brick building embracing one corner of a spacious quadrangle on a campus that looks transplanted whole from the Midwest, with austere buildings and perennial borders and a little stream with ducks. I'd competently met her roommate and her roommate's parents, helped her set up a bank account, fussed with her computer, stood in line with her as she registered. All these blessed details occupied my mind, so I didn't have time to think about the moment when we would drive away and leave her here.

My first tears came at the convocation, as the organist played a hymn from my childhood: "Our Father, by whose name." I sang the words in my mind:

"Bless all our children, loving well,
"With constant love the sentinel,
"The homes in which thy people dwell."

Is it here, the edge of her childhood? In my mind I saw her back home, this last summer. Faithfully every morning she'd stretch her long legs and pull on her shoes and set out eastward along Elkins Road, running toward the sun, her ponytail swaying behind her. Many mornings I'd stand at the kitchen window, holding a cup of coffee, and watch as she disappeared into the golden light. Her figure receded, getting smaller, smaller, and then I would blink and she would be gone.

My dad used to tell a joke about a man who insisted on driving his car backwards. Someone asked him, "How can you see where you're going?" The man replied, "I can't, but I have a dandy view of where I've been." It seems to me that we humans have eyes in the backs of our hearts. We're better at knowing where we've been than where we're going. So we borrow rituals from our ancestors, mark our transitions with mileposts of one kind and another. The newspaper gives us the exact moment of sunrise, and when people go fishing they consult tide charts printed with numbers like "7:43 a.m."

I wonder if all our measuring and marking isn't a big sham, born of a wistful hope that pinning something down is the same thing as controlling it. With the right mathematics you can figure out the exact moment when the tide turns, or when the sun comes up. But who ever sees it happening? You are in a familiar landscape and then you blink and everything looks different.

So I don't know exactly when it happened. But I do know this: at the beginning of that convocation service, our daughter belonged to us, and at the end she belonged to herself, to Whitman College, and to the world. As the organist pealed out the triumphal strains of a Bach chorale, we rose, we suddenly vestigial parents, and applauded the Class of 2002.

Kindling

❧❧

On winter Sundays I fill the woodbox. We heat the upstairs with a small woodstove that came from the dealer in Model T black. We painted it blue to resemble the woodstove we really wanted but couldn't afford, a high-legged, angular Jøtul with a baked-on cobalt finish and, on its side, a bas-relief sculpture of a young man playing a guitar to a naked woods nymph sunning herself at his feet. Our friends Alex and Lynn have that model, and one day, says Lynn, a visitor gazed at the side of their stove and then said fervently, "I wish I could play the guitar like that!" Our stove is a sturdy Franklin with an ample firebox and curvy Queen Anne legs, and the casting on its side shows a pony approaching a log cabin under a tall fir tree.

Our stove needs two cords of wood plus kindling to keep the upstairs warm all winter. For cordwood we use chunks of apple and pear, from when we culled the orchard, and pine and fir thinnings from the overgrown Christmas-tree patch Grandpa put in forty years ago. What we call the woodshed was once the chicken house, and then it was an open-sided workshop where Bob, my mother's boyfriend, cast the concrete footings for a shop to work on the gravestones he carved for a living. Then it was a pigpen, then a manger where we bottle-fed two bummer lambs through cold spring nights. Now it's a tractor garage. The firewood shares the rent with the tractor, which gets covered with sawdust and chips during the winter.

Our kindling, too, comes from several layers back in our past. Long ago, years before John and I moved here, Dad would visit Mom from time to time, hoping perhaps to patch things up between them. One time he came down with a load of cedar shingles he'd gotten in some barter deal and put them up on the inside of the basement family room. It was an unusual way to finish a room, but I guess the shingles were an improvement over the bleak concrete of the inside foundation wall. When John and I moved in, we lived with the shingles. I used a stiff broom to knock the cobwebs and dust as best I could off their rough ridges, but those walls were impossible to keep clean. One day I pulled them down and patched and painted the concrete underneath. Until we nail up furring strips and do a proper drywalling, I think I like the concrete better, although it's a tossup sometimes.

Anyway, it's too late now, because the shingles went onto the kindling pile. Next to them is a stack of tongue-and-groove that used to be the living-room walls. This old schoolhouse was built before plywood was invented, before sheetrock was even dreamed of. Over the wall studs—unplaned, clear, full-dimension two-by-fours—the builder had fitted clear fir tongue-and-groove and then pasted on construction paper. The walls were finished with wallpaper, several layers of it over the years. When we moved in, the top layer of wallpaper was a tan grasscloth reminiscent of the inside of a tiki restaurant. Grandpa had put it up in the fifties, when *South Pacific* and *Blue Hawaii* were on everybody's minds. When we got ready to redo the living room, John ripped it down only to realize that the motley shreds of wallpaper and construction paper were going to leave the wall impossible to finish. There was nothing to do but saw out the tongue-and-groove. So now it sits in fifteen-inch lengths on the kindling pile, and still clinging to some of the boards are strips of wallpaper bearing delicate sprigs of violet or starchy Oxford stripes.

I seized a length of tongue-and-groove and went to work with the hatchet. It split beautifully, knotless ancient wood, layer upon taut layer of perfectly even grain. I'll bet this tree was four hundred years old, I thought to myself. Whack whack whack: each blow sheared a half-inch flitch off the edge, sending up a spicy resinous odor that I recognized instantly as the smell of Grandma's house. Old pitch softened in the summer, congealed again in the winter, a golden smell, mellow as amber, vaporized at the blow of the axe. I smell its vague perfume still when I stand in my closet—Grandma's closet—on a warm day.

A blow to the senses can break open a scene locked for years in the amber resin of memory. The smells of roasting wieners and watermelon wilting in the sun always take me back to the Elks picnic at the Cooston grange hall, when Daddy swung me in a swing so high, so high, grabbing my ankles and pulling hard, and at the top of the orbit the ropes slackened and for a second, for an eternity, I floated weightless.

It doesn't have to be a smell. Sometimes a glimpse of something so ephemeral it seems like nothing at all will whack loose the image of a man rowing a boat up a narrow creek through the dunes, of a family eating s'mores and laughing in a picnic shelter in the pouring rain, of a strawberry-haired young woman, a stranger to me but I couldn't take my eyes off her, sitting at an outdoor table unbraiding her hair, sending an amber river rippling down her back, combing it out with her fingers, her fingers knowing what her eyes couldn't see.

I came to visit my mother once when my father was there, not long after he had shingled the basement. We sat in front of the fireplace. I chattered away about college and boys, probably— I don't remember. He listened, nodded, asked me a gentle question now and then. His big hands fed leftover shards of cedar into the fire, and the flames leaped up and painted the dark walls strawberry-gold. He and Mom never did get back together, but there were many acts of practical tenderness between them, right up to the end. What seems a ruined life may be, from time to time, illuminated by flickers of an almost unbearable sweetness.

As I loaded up the wheelbarrow, it occurred to me that we were burning up the house to keep the house warm. I was momentarily discomfited by the thought. In fact, I felt a little horrified, as at the sight of an animal gnawing its leg off to escape a trap, or a woman dieting so severely that her body consumes its own muscle tissue. But then I realized it isn't like that, really. Splitting that wood and smelling its sharp smell gave me a happy feeling, purposeful and thrifty. The old wood has done its job. What better use for it now than to be transformed into warmth and memory? It's more like putting manure on the vegetable garden. It's more like salmon dying and rotting all along the rivers, their life force spent, their death-force feeding the fungi that feed the plants that feed the bugs that feed the young fish, and everything going on in a continuous story, no beginning, no end.

Home for Thanksgiving

❧❧

This year it was my turn to have the family home for Thanksgiving. When I was a child, Grandma did it every year, and we all just assumed we were invited, Grandma and Grandpa's five sons and daughters and their spouses, seventeen grandchildren, and sometimes Grandpa's two sisters and their husbands and a few of their children.

My family always drove up from Coos Bay, a six-hour trip back then before there were freeways. My three sisters and I would fuss and whine in the car, but we'd also sing "Over the River and Through the Woods" in four-part harmony. To Grandmother's house we went, and for us it was the best holiday of the year, better than Christmas.

The house was bursting with relatives. The uncles hung around the long table, visiting, with long pauses in between sentences, or they stood outside in the rain, smoking. Grandma and the aunts pulled in their stomachs and sidled past one another in the tiny kitchen, carrying casseroles of creamed onions and glazed sweet potatoes in oven-mitted hands. The windows steamed up, and the air was hot and fumy with turkey and tobacco smoke. We children stole up the basement stairs in our stocking feet to spy on the grownups and then ran whooping back down. Or else we went outside to break the ice on the pond with our rubber boots, or (later) light furtive cigarettes out behind the chicken house.

The Thanksgiving memories jumble together. I remember one where my uncle Stan, a man of black moods and rages, was in a rare good humor and said, in a stage whisper, as the turkey was making its entrance, "I think there's a dead bird on this table." My aunt later divorced him, and much later Uncle Stan shot himself, having mailed his suicide note to his younger son.

But there was joy at these gatherings. We sang "Praise God, From Whom All Blessings Flow" around the table. Afterward we sat with stomachs distended, stunned with food. And then we roused ourselves and made music: Mom on the trombone, Auntie Ann on the piano, Uncle Stan singing in his splendid baritone voice, their sons Heintz and Dietrich on the clarinet and the violin, me on the flute, Cousin Mike on the trumpet.

All the Thompson adults eventually divorced, but before that, before my parents' marriage broke up, before my father succumbed to the ravages of throat cancer and late-stage alcoholism, he could tell funny stories. He told this story about one Thanksgiving that had been more of a strain than usual: Our family was the last to leave. My mother and father and my sisters and I climbed into our Chevy station wagon to go back to Coos Bay. The car had been having engine problems, and as Dad slid behind the wheel, he heard Grandpa say to Grandma—standing there on the porch, she smoothing back her hair, he waving kindly—he swore Grandpa leaned over to Grandma and murmured, "Gawd, I hope it starts."

These days the family is smaller and more scattered. Grandma: dead of a stroke in 1966. My father, cancer and chronic alcoholism, 1984. Grandpa, lung disease, 1985. Uncle Stan, suicide, about 1986. Aunt Timmy, unspecified causes aggravated by chronic alcoholism, about 1987. Aunt Patsy and Aunt Maxie, Grandpa's sisters, still living but frail. Uncle Paul, my mother's oldest brother, wintering in Palm Springs in his fifth-wheeler, a wandering hermit and liking it that way. My sister Melinda, coping with schizophrenia with the help of medication, doing very well in her little world but unable to face a family gathering.

Because this house was Grandma's house, I felt burdened, when we first moved here, with the expectation that I should keep up the annual family Thanksgiving. I couldn't manage it; it was just too hard. Hard, naturally, to pull together a party every year for twenty-five or thirty people, but more than that, hard to feel I had to be the solid center of the family, to feel the family was depending on me to provide this ritual meal. But like most burdens, this one was also a blessing. After a while—I'm not sure how it happened—I got so I could invite the family home for Thanksgiving every few years. That felt manageable.

∽◯∽

This year we had fourteen people, including John, Gavin, Mary, and me. The house was pleasantly full, not crammed the way it used to be. And for the first time since we moved here I was working in a kitchen with a level floor—something most people take for granted, but for me it was a great gift.

The weekend before, John had rented a floor jack and jacked up the northeast corner of the kitchen a full five and a half inches. That was quite a distance when you consider that the kitchen is only ten feet long. That corner had been sinking for years. The drainage has always been poor there, and over the years water had collected every winter and undermined the foundation. Which, like everything else in this house, was in tough shape to start with.

Several years ago we thought the kitchen had finished settling. John installed new cabinets and shimmed them to level. But it wasn't finished settling, and the floor and the countertops continued to sink, although at slightly different angles. We were used to leaning to the left as we headed toward the basement door. Water had always run north on the countertop, puddling under the blender and the coffeepot.

Now the kitchen was suddenly, startlingly level, and I found myself tripping over bare linoleum. The water on the counter reversed itself like tidewater backing up into an estuary, flowing south to puddle under the radio and the toaster.

The leveling seemed to startle the house, too. Diagonal rips appeared in the kitchen wallpaper, and the window frames, wrenched into right angles, separated a bit from their sockets, leaving stiletto-shaped voids. The windows didn't break, though—the wooden frames are so old and loose that the glass just shifted inside its grooves. In another house this degree of slop might be regarded as a liability, but in our house it's an asset. Flexibility may be more important than strength in the long run.

Another thing that happened was that the rainwater reversed its flow on the kitchen's roof, and on Thanksgiving morning there was a leak where there had been none before. John climbed up onto the roof, slid on his belly under the main roof overhang to get at the leak, and goobered the surface with tar. Inside, I put bowls under the drips, glad I didn't need the bowls for Thanksgiving dinner.

Nobody noticed the ripped wallpaper or the cracks around the window frames. My family is used to this house, used to something always being makeshift or out of kilter. There's always a patch or a rip or a bucket underneath some leak. It's always been that way, ever since Grandpa took this ruined old schoolhouse and made a home out of it. Among his many changes, Grandpa took the second story off the schoolhouse and slapped on a slanted shed roof. I wish he'd left the second story. It was rickety, but it did have a pitched roof—I've seen the old pictures. In this wet country, an almost-flat roof is just asking for trouble. So the house has always leaked. It leaked when my grandparents lived here; it leaked when my mother lived here; and every winter for fifteen years John and I and the kids stepped over buckets.

Four years ago John and I took off the roof and put a new one on. We tore off the old rolled asphalt roofing and the tarpaper and the tongue-and-groove laps, laying the top of the house bare right down to the rafters. We shoveled out the vermiculite and the blown-in cellulose insulation, full of mouse turds and board ends, and spread it on the garden. We rebuilt the rotten corners with two-by-sixes and new faschia trim. We shimmed up the sagging rafters in the middle of the house, reflashed around the chimneys, nailed down plywood sheeting, rolled out roofing, and sealed it with tar.

At the most vulnerable point in this process, after the old roof was off but before we had the new plywood down, there was a summer storm, one of those flash squalls that delivers a flood out of a clear blue sky. We scrambled to spread plastic sheeting over the rafters, stapling it taut so the water would run off. We almost won the race. The plastic kept most of the water out, but a little came into the kitchen and the dining room, and now we have stains in the ceiling to remember it by.

Reroofing was a hard job. I nailed plywood and rolled tarpaper till my fingertips were numb and my elbow tendon screaming.

Still, it must have been much easier for us than it was for my grandfather. He and Uncle Ralph and my father put down the old roof with tongue-and-groove, one piece at a time, laboriously cutting the ends to fit. Our six dozen sheets of plywood went down pretty fast, even though John had to measure and cut them to fit the rafters, which (no surprise) are spaced irregularly.

It is so much easier to fix things with the right materials and the right tools. When Mom and Dad were struggling with Dad's alcoholism and Melinda's schizophrenia, they had to make the best of a really bad situation, and they didn't have much wisdom or sympathy to help them. We pretended to be a normal family then, because that was all we knew how to do. Maybe "pretended" is too harsh. We really *tried* to be a normal family. But we weren't strong enough. Such love and caring as we could muster had to be stretched around Dad's and my sister's inexplicable ways, and around the compensatory reactions of the rest of us, and sometimes there was just not enough to stretch.

Now I have better tools. A deeper understanding of addiction and mental illness. A husband who is strong and good. Healthy children. A spirit of optimism that seems to flow in when I stir myself to improve something. A bit more compassion, a bit more courage, a bit more wisdom.

Three-year-old nephew Lucas, Leslie's youngest, wants to help fix Thanksgiving dinner, so I set the potato kettle on the floor and put him to work with the masher. I step over him to stir the gravy. There is too much food, there are too many willing hands to help. It is too hot and too noisy and there is no room in the kitchen. I smile and surrender and let the meal unfold: turkey dressing mashed potatoes gravy cranberry sauce rolls green beans creamed onions leek soup Waldorf salad pickled herring Jell-O with mandarin oranges yams with marshmallows ... We are an hour late sitting down.

We sing "Praise God" around the table, our voices rippling raggedly through the harmony. After dinner we say, "It's *hot* in here!" and open the doors, and Heintz and Dietrich play folk songs on the dobro bass and the guitar, and Gavin plays fiery, fast-fingered blues, and Mary sings "Georgia On My Mind." I whip the cream for the pie, two whole pints in a big bowl. Lucas licks the beaters.

Then I sit down with coffee and pie and an ache in my lower back. The muscles soften, the tension drains. I am happy. Everybody is happy. I am startled to realize it. I'm not sure how it happened, but my vision of my troubled family has shifted like a window frame being jacked into square. At least for today, everything is right.

Country Property

≈≈

Our children came home for Labor Day weekend, Gavin to help his dad patch the carport roof, Mary to shop for a wedding dress.

"If we're ever going to sell this house, or even rent it out," John had said to me the night before, "we'll need to take care of those carport leaks once and for all."

I smiled to myself. We say that every time we patch that roof, but somehow the roof doesn't get the message. "Maybe you could talk to Gavin about designing a deck, too?" I said. For years we had been planning to put a deck on the east side of the house, ever since we tore the old rotten one off fifteen years ago.

"We've got an architect son," said John. "Might as well take advantage of it."

"We'll never be able to sell this place with those terrible old steps out there," I said.

Sell this place. John and I had been dancing with that question for a decade, teasing ourselves with it, scaring ourselves with it.

We'd start by agreeing on the plain facts. This house is too big, too drafty, and too far from town. It's too much work: a garden, an orchard, a vineyard, and a woodlot. It's too empty with the children gone.

Then we'd slip into fantasy. What would it be like to walk to the store instead of driving? To step out the door onto a sidewalk instead of a muddy gravel driveway? To turn a thermostat when we wanted heat, instead of pulling on barn boots and a slicker and gloves and grabbing the ax on the way out to the woodshed? What would it be like to live in a place uninhabited by spirits, a place where memories don't seep out of the walls?

While John and Gavin unrolled and hammered asphalt roofing, Mary and I went shopping. She and Troy are aiming for a July wedding, depending on the availability of hotel ballrooms, seasonal flowers, and time off from her banker's job. She already has her lists, my practical daughter: Find Venue, Interview

Photographers, Costco Cake?, Bridesmaids' Dresses, Tux for Troy? Or Dark Suit?

The woman at the bridal shop brought her dress after dress to try on. They all looked nice, but she and I agreed that the frothy, frou-frou ones didn't do much for her tall frame and aquiline features. In the end she chose a plain princess-cut strapless sheath with an overskirt of subtly worked lace. As she emerged from the dressing room radiant as a goddess, I suddenly saw my eight-year-old Mary in pink satin and tulle and ballet slippers, a beautiful girl ready to dance.

I was never one for froth and frou-frou either. My wedding dress, sewn by my mother, was even plainer than Mary's, with tight sleeves and a high, modest neckline. I muffled a gasp as I looked at the dress's price tag. "Don't worry, Mom," Mary said. "Troy and I can take care of this."

We came home to find John and Gavin drinking beer at the table in their tar-stained clothes. Gavin was sketching a deck design. His big hand wielded the pencil deftly, floating the point across the page, laying down the picture in his mind's eye, marking corners with precise angles and perfect perspective. Gavin was a rambunctious two-year-old when we brought him to this house. We hadn't been here three weeks when, racing headlong across the deck that is now gone, he fell down the steps and put a gash in his forehead. My children are grownups now, competent and skillful. I don't know why that amazes me, but it does.

Later, over red snapper and garden tomatoes, we talk about this house. It's the same dithering conversation we've been having for the past few years now, but lately the urgency seems to be building. "What if we rented it out?" I said, thinking it was a way to put our toes in the water without committing ourselves to the plunge.

Gavin thought renting was a bad idea. "You have to think about the kind of people who would want to rent a place like this," he said. "Sorry, Mom, but it won't be people like you and

Dad. They'd go buy a house somewhere, probably a better house than this one. Sorry, Dad. I know you've worked hard on this place, but it's not in that great shape, let's face it."

We know, I thought. *That's why we're talking about this.*

"The only people you'll get are college kids who'll want to go down in the woods and party and maybe burn the place down. I know what they're like," he added. "I used to be one of them."

"You should just put it on the market," said Mary. "Country property is hot right now."

Yes, but … Yes, but … "But it still needs so much work," I said.

"Gail," John said, "it always needs work. It needs endless work. Remember?"

"So don't fix it up," Mary said. "Sell it at a discount. You'll still get a good price. You'd be surprised at what properties like this are going for on the Internet."

What do you mean, "properties"? Why aren't you all crying about this?

As if hearing my thoughts, Gavin said, "I have to admit, I feel a little bit of nostalgia for the place. It was a great place to grow up. And I've had dreams of some day bringing my kids back here, back to Grandma's house, like you did, Mom." He smiled, and I felt a catch in my throat. "But the place is too much for you. I can see that. I don't want you to hang onto it and work yourselves to death."

"Don't worry, Mom," said Mary, for the second time that day. "We had a wonderful childhood here. Now we're grown up. You can let it go."

The day before, I'd walked down to the orchard to pick up some windfalls to make applesauce. Our Jon Grimes tree typically drops its fruit all at once. You have to catch it before it lets the apples go, or you get nothing but windfalls. I never catch it before it lets the apples go.

I stooped, brushing aside the yellowjackets, and tossed apples into the bucket: bruised apples, wormy apples, scabby apples, each with a little sound flesh left, something that made it redeemable. *Why didn't we prune these trees last winter?* I thought. I looked up through the tangled branches and realized with perfect clarity that we were not going to prune them this winter, either. We will never prune these trees again. We will never put a pitched roof on the house. We will never saw our fir trees into lumber and build a deck on the east side. We will never build raised beds; we will never have a well-tended vineyard. We will never plant a woodland garden in the brush-choked strip across the creek.

There was a time when the promises I made to myself were enough to keep me going. I can still see my woodland garden in my mind's eye: a path crossing a little bridge and winding through rhododendron, vine maple, crabapple, dogwood, and willow, with trillium and tigerlily at my feet, and wild ginger and evergreen huckleberry.

I picked up an apple that was mostly rotten and felt my thumb sink into the slimy hole. I threw it hard at the trunk of the tree. It splatted shreds of brown pulp back at me. I picked up another apple and threw it at the tree, and another, and another, harder and harder. Pretty soon the trunk had a sticky brown bull's-eye, and curious yellowjackets were starting to nose around it. I stopped and caught my breath, wiped my hand on my overalls, wiped my knuckles across my eyes.

I don't want to prune these trees any more. I don't want to saw my own lumber and build my own deck. I don't want a woodland garden. Twenty-five years ago I wanted these things. Now I don't. Is that a crime?

After dinner I offered applesauce, but John said, "No. We're going to town to get ice cream." So we piled into the car the way we used to do when the kids were little, except now Gavin had to fold his six-foot-two frame into the backseat of the Subaru, and Mary sat with her knees practically to her chin.

Just like we used to do, we drove the seven miles to the grocery store in Independence. "All right, what kind does everybody want?" John said, as he always did, hovering over the frozen-foods case. "Chocolate Chip Mint, Oregon Blueberry, Chunky Monkey, Brown Cow?" In the end we chose vanilla, as we always do, plus chocolate syrup and caramel sauce and whipped cream and bananas. Then we crammed ourselves into the car and drove home and feasted on banana splits one more time, a celebration and a wake.

Everything Must Go

❧❧

Strangers are prowling through my house, fingering bowls full of cookie cutters, stacks of mismatched plates, camp chairs with torn webbing. Unfolding and folding bedsheets, inspecting stuffed animals, lifting the lids of board games with pieces missing. I am holed up in the kitchen, clutching my cash box, protected from the rummagers by a sign: "No Sale Items in Kitchen."

Two women are picking things up and putting them down as they converse softly in Spanish. A mixing bowl. A styrofoam Thanksgiving decoration in the shape of a cornucopia. A sackful of curling irons. One comes up to me with a stuffed tiger-striped neck pillow that I bought at O'Hare Airport two years ago. Its sticker says "$2."

"One dollar?" she asks.

"Sure." She dumps a handful of change into my hand and walks away smiling. I'm happy, too. That neck pillow wasn't worth the nine dollars and ninety-nine cents I paid for it, and it was a nuisance to carry through the airport. But here it is, still taking up space in my life. I'm glad to see it go.

A man squats down next to the kitchen door to examine four ancient 220-volt heaters. He wanders away, comes back and squats again, runs his hand over the grille, fingers the frayed fabric around the cord, debates with himself. "These things work?" he asks. He has gray hair, a hard face. He speaks out of the left side of his mouth, as if the right side were permanently reserved for a cigarette.

"Some of them have an element burned out," I tell him. "Here, plug this one in and try." He plugs it in, and presently the right element glows red, but the left side stays dark. "Prob'ly too old to get parts for," the man says.

"Most likely," I say. "But maybe they have antique value." The man humphs and wanders off.

Those heaters were once the sole source of warmth for this house. Before John and I put in the woodstove, before we put in the pellet furnace, back when the kids were babies, this house was cold and damp most of the time. I have no nostalgia for those heaters.

Our ad in Friday's paper said: "Leaving Farmhouse After 25 Years. Everything Must Go." We'd spent the previous week hauling stuff out of closets: bundled fabric remnants, bent ski poles, orphaned knitting needles, coffee cans full of keys, Mason jars with chipped rims, five-gallon buckets with the handles missing, plastic bags of twistums for closing plastic bags—all the things you keep just because you can, if you live in a big old house.

We tackled the basement storeroom with its family knickknacks and oddities. Some of them had been there since my grandparents' day: the silk parachute Grandpa brought back from the war, the Japanese flash cards, the Chinese paper kite, the round-bellied Matrioshka dolls he and Grandma had picked up on their travels. The Give Away pile got bigger, and so did the Throw Away pile.

The hardest things to face were the boxes of Gavin's and Mary's stuff, their schoolwork and sports mementos from kindergarten through college. I resolved to be choosy, like an efficient museum curator. I would keep the best (Gavin's spaceship drawings, Mary's stories) and let the rest go. But it was too hard. I couldn't muster enough dispassionate judgment. I had to blink back the tears and just power through it. This stays. This, this, this, and this goes.

"We don't have to do this," John and I would remind each other when both of us got to sniffling. "We're leaving this place because we want to." *Yes,* I told myself. *Yes, we are.*

❧❧

Before seven o'clock on the morning of the sale, cars had started to line up along Elkins Road. People stood in our driveway with their hands jammed into their pockets, eyeing the door. John stationed himself in the carport to handle the tools and garden things. When I opened the door at eight o'clock, there was a rush. Pretty soon I saw people walking back to their cars clutching their change and their treasures: a wooden three-legged stool with a cracked seat, a bent aluminum stepladder. I was suddenly put in mind of a thousand ants scattering from a mound of food, each bearing a crumb.

It's a complicated thing, watching people walk away with pieces of your life. On the one hand it feels a little obscene, exposing my private memories to a bunch of strangers. But everything touches off a memory, everything is meaningful, and you can't hang onto every little piece. It's better to let things go, give them to people who can get some use out of them. Isn't it? It's recycling; that's what I tell myself.

As we've explained this move to our friends, several have said, "Oh, no! You're leaving the family place? How can you?" I say—I keep hearing myself say—that the treasures that have sustained me in my quarter-century in this place are with me still, not in the house but in my head and my heart.

And yet, objects can be soaked in meaning, and not all of it can be extracted and made portable. This house sits here, brooding and powerful, alive with history. Our family stories have haunted the place the whole time we've been here, or so it has felt to me. A place of enchantment is not always a pleasant home. History is as full of pain and tragedy as it is of delight and joy.

Right now I don't want to feel it, the pain or the joy, either one. I don't want to feel anything. This house is now an object, a thing apart from myself. A property.

A woman comes to the kitchen door and looks covetously at Grandma's schoolhouse clock. "That's not for sale," I say. "We're taking that with us."

"I would, too," she says, and picks up a cookie tin full of crayons.

The man who had been looking at the heaters reappears and hands me two hundred-dollar bills. "Your husband sold me the tractor," he says, nodding his head out the east window. "8N. Five hundred. Bring the rest of the money when I come get it tomorrow."

Another man comes up to me and shakes my hand and says, "I knew your grandfather when he lived here. I was in his math class in college. He was the best teacher I ever had. He knew how to explain things very thoroughly."

"Yes, I know," I say, remembering Grandpa's interminable stories about his ancestors. Then, feeling a pang of guilt, I say, "He was a wonderful grandpa, and I always loved visiting him and Grandma here."

"So, you're letting the place go out of the family?"

Yes, but it's not like you think. Grandpa was the least sentimental man in the world. He'd be fine with it. My mother approves, too. Anyway, why do I need to defend myself to this stranger? "I have the family's permission," I say, smiling.

I came back on Sunday to cart the leftover stuff to the Goodwill. The man who'd bought the tractor was there with two other men. They were laboriously winching it onto a lowboy trailer. Its enormous wheels wouldn't clear the trailer's wheel wells, so the men unbolted one tractor wheel, shimmed the axle with a thick piece of firewood, and then rolled the loose wheel forward and laid it on its side on the front of the trailer—an ingenious solution, I thought. Then they winched the tractor the rest of the way on, its axle skidding forward on the wood. I watched in silence as they worked. After the tractor was chained down, the man handed me fifteen twenty-dollar bills. I took the money into the house and wrapped it in a dishtowel and put it in the freezer, the way Dad used to do whenever he had money. Cold cash, he called it.

For the next couple of hours I carted boxes down to the carport. By the time John arrived, the living room was empty except for the piano and the sofa. We loaded the boxes into both cars. Then we went back in to pick up the money and lock up. It had been cold all day, and now it was getting dark. We turned off the lights and surveyed the room.

"Well, we're down to the piano and the couch," I said.

"Gavin's coming down next weekend to help with the piano," said John.

"Yes. And Wade and Karen are taking the couch."

"Yep. And we have to get the last of the stuff out of the storeroom."

"Right. And then I'll clean this place from top to bottom."

"So, one more trip up."

"And then we'll be done."

"That'll be good."

We looked at each other, and our faces crumpled. We embraced each other, held each other, and wept for a long moment.

"Well," said John, wiping his eyes. "I guess this is harder than we thought."

"But it's the right thing," I said.

"Yes," said John. "It is the right thing."

Then we locked the front door and drove in our separate cars home to town.

Moving the Piano

〜〜

The piano mover offered us a choice. He would bring his crew and move the piano for six hundred dollars. Or he would build us a "skid," as he called it, and show John how to use it, for two hundred dollars. Providing the muscle and the piano dolly would then be up to us.

I envisioned a big boxy thing, like a piano coffin, but the skid proved to be a four-foot-long, eight-inch-wide slab of carpet-coated plywood with a two-by-four nailed to each long edge. It looked like a bed for a long, skinny dog. The two-by-fours had holes drilled in them to accommodate nylon straps.

I was dubious. The thing looked flimsy, inadequate for moving a seven-hundred-pound baby grand.

"No, it's a great tool," said John. "He showed me how to use it. Gavin and I can do this easily." The technique called for gravity and leverage, he said, not brute force. The piano mover's parting words had been, "Remember—a piano is not worth a person." In other words, if it starts to go, let it go.

John and Gavin circled the piano like prizefighters as John explained the technique. "Okay, okay, Dad, I've got it," Gavin said, more than once.

"Yeah, well, this is important, so just give me a moment of your precious time, will you?" said John.

After he was finished explaining, he unscrewed the pedal column and took it off. Then he placed the skid on the floor, aligning it carefully with the piano's long left edge. With Gavin bracing the piano, he unscrewed the left front leg, and the two of them lowered the left edge onto the waiting skid. They removed the other two legs and tipped the body up so that it rested on its edge, and then they strapped it securely to the skid. John rocked the skid forward, and Gavin slid the piano dolly underneath, and John tipped it back up, and there was our piano, ready to roll. On its side it looked like a whale on a barge, something large and helpless and tied down, being taken somewhere not of its choosing.

The floor where the piano had stood was filmed with dust. I found the broom and swept the linoleum twice, then washed it with a wet rag. Later I would clean the whole house: scrub the baseboards, wash down the walls, mop the floors, scour the sinks and toilets, wipe out the cabinets, polish the windows. "Why don't you hire it done?" my mother asked me. I told her I'd think about it, but the truth was, I didn't want to leave this final chore to a stranger. I guess I needed to know my hands would be giving this house its last touches.

As John and Gavin were laying the piano on the skid, my sister arrived from Ashland with the horse trailer, swept of its manury straw to receive the piano. The piano is going to my niece Emily, Leslie's daughter, until we have a house again. Brother-in-law Michael backed the trailer expertly up to the front steps. "Emily is ecstatic about getting the piano!" said my sister, giving me her usual exuberant hug. "Come on, I want to look at your new bathroom again."

We walked into the basement and gazed at John's latest handiwork, the stylish little bathroom where the old smelly one used to be, with a new shower and a glass-brick wall and a toilet firmly planted to the floor.

"It looks like he patched the holes in the walls, too," Leslie said. "I remember some nights when I'd get up to go to the bathroom and have to fight a raccoon for the toilet paper."

There was plenty of muscle to move the piano. They wouldn't need me for a while, so I slipped away for one last turn around the place. I walked south along the creek, next to the chest-high billow of Himalaya blackberry. How many hours had I spent whacking that tide of stickers with the machete? And what do I have to show for it? Scratch-scars all over my arms, yes, but also jewel-jars of jam, musky and blue-black, with seeds that crunch and juice that stains your teeth.

I could hear the creek tumbling behind the tangle of brambles. *What does this feel like?* I asked myself.

It feels like coming to the end of a long indentured servitude, that's what it feels like.

I entered the dim sunlight of the glade. When I was a child, there were three ancient oak trees here. Grandpa hung a swing from the lowest branch of the middle oak, twenty feet above the ground. After Thanksgiving dinners we grandkids would troop down to the glade, if it wasn't pouring rain, and take turns swinging. The big kids would push the little kids, and the little kids would clutch the ropes as our bottoms slid back and forth on the wide plank seat. I remembered my cousin Alan pushing me in the swing, and when I swung up past his head he'd yank on my ankles to push me even higher on the forward arc.

What does this feel like?

It feels like putting up a child for adoption.

I rounded the southwest corner. The afternoon sun was coming in, and I could see the neighbor's field through a gap in the brush. There used to be a plank bridge leading to Grandma's woodland garden across the creek. The plank was gone, rotted away, and now there was only a blown-down cottonwood tree. Grandma used to clear patches for the wildflowers back there, fawn lily, wild iris, and trillium. They still came up each spring, poking themselves into a willow thicket crowned with downed tree limbs and choked with blackberry vines. I scrambled up the cottonwood log and sat for a while.

What does this feel like?

It feels like flunking a grade in school.

I walked into Grandpa's woods. The Christmas trees he planted forty years ago were a forest of towering poles, half of them leaning against their neighbors. Here Gavin and Mary used to poke through the duff to find owl pellets, and Gavin and his friends played Capture-the-Flag.

I rounded the low southeast corner and came up through the orchard. Grandpa's prune trees still produced a meager crop each fall, neglected though they were. The apples were more generous. They'd given us countless quarts of applesauce, countless gallons of cider. Not this year, though.

What does this feel like?

It feels like being scolded for ingratitude.

I walked into the vineyard. It was our vineyard; we'd planted it ourselves. It didn't come from my grandparents or my mother. I stooped and yanked handfuls of quackgrass from between the vines, twisted off a clump of almost-ripe grapes and crammed them into my mouth. They tasted tart and sweet.

What does this feel like?

It feels like being pulled up by the roots.

Up behind the house I walked past the bay window that John built in our bedroom wall. We'd had to sleep in the dining room while John finished that window. But then on summer nights we could open the window and let in the sounds of the dark, coyotes keening, mourning doves crying, spring peepers shrilling. I peered in the window and saw an empty room with boxes on the floor.

What does this feel like?

It feels like a divorce.

How many nails had we hammered into this house? How many weary high-fives as the last coat of paint went on? How many sheets of drywall? How many evenings curled up next to the woodstove? How many Christmas mornings? How many acres of asphalt roofing? How many family picnics? How many buckets under leaks? How many nights wrapped up snug in bed listening to the wind howl down the chimney?

Goodbye, house. We've had quite a time, haven't we?

What does this feel like?

It feels like the end of the world.

It feels like freedom.

Dry-eyed, I slipped back through the carport just as the men were easing the piano up the cardboard ramp into the trailer. Leslie and I laid a horse blanket over it, and Michael and John snugged it to the trailer's side with the straps. Then Michael backed the trailer out onto Elkins Road, and we waved, and they waved, and then the driveway was empty except for our car.

"Come on," said John, taking my hand. "Let's go home."